cook's library

Fish & Seafood

cook's library
Fish & Seafood

p

This is a Parragon Publishing Book
This edition published in 2004

Parragon Publishing
Queen Street House
4 Queen Street
Bath BA1 1HE, UK

ISBN: 0-75259-445-1

Printed in China

NOTE

Cup measurements in this book are for American cups. This book
uses imperial and metric measurements. Follow the same units of
measurement throughout; do not mix imperial and metric. All spoon
measurements are level: teaspoons are assumed to be 5 ml,
and tablespoons are assumed to be 15 ml. Unless otherwise stated,
milk is assumed to be full fat, eggs and individual vegetables such
as potatoes are medium, and pepper is freshly ground black pepper.

The times given for each recipe are an approximate guide only because
the preparation times may differ according to the techniques used by
different people and the cooking times may vary as a result of the type
of oven used. The preparation times include chilling and marinating
times, where appropriate.

Recipes using raw or very lightly cooked eggs should be avoided
by infants, the elderly, pregnant women, convalescents, and anyone
suffering from an illness.

Contents

Introduction

Seafood rightly deserves its image as a healthy food. It is high in protein and has the added bonus that oily fish, such as mackerel and herring, is high in polyunsaturated fatty acid (omega-3)—the fat that helps reduce cholesterol levels. White fish are a good source of minerals as well as being low in fat, especially if poached, steamed, or lightly broiled. Although shellfish have been linked with high cholesterol, they are also low in saturated fats and are therefore fine eaten in moderation.

The sheer variety of fish and shellfish is staggering. If you decided to eat seafood just once a week, you could go for a whole year without eating the same dish twice. Seafood is also quick and easy to prepare, making it an attractive ingredient to the busy cook. Often sold ready to cook, fish can be prepared in minutes, and most shellfish is sold already cooked, needing even less preparation.

Fish is also better value for money than meat, because there is much less waste. Making fish a regular part of your diet makes a lot of sense.

Buying Fish and Shellfish

Wherever you are shopping for fish, at your local trusted fish market or supermarket, the guidelines are the same:

- The eyes of the fish should be clear, bright, and moist. Fish with dull, gray, or cloudy eyes should be avoided.

- The gills of the fish should be bright red or pink, not dull and gray.

- The fish should smell of the sea and nothing else.

- If you press the fish lightly with your thumb, the flesh should spring back, leaving little or no imprint.

- The shells of hinged shellfish, such as oysters, mussels, and clams, should be tightly closed prior to cooking. If they are slightly open, tap them sharply. If they do not close, discard them.

- Cooked shellfish should smell fresh, with no hint of ammonia. If available, check the expiration date.

Snacks *and* Appetizers

The dishes in this chapter are designed either as appetizers for the main course to come or as snacks to serve with drinks. Fish and seafood make excellent appetizers as they are full of flavor and can be turned into a variety of delicious dishes.

Fish cooks quickly, making it ideal for entertaining. Many of the dishes in this chapter can be prepared in advance and served cold, such as the Anchovy Bites, the Smoked Mackerel Pâté, and the Lime and Basil Cured Salmon.

There is a wide selection to suit all tastes, for example the Thai Crab Omelet, Potted Shrimp, and Maryland Crab Cakes with a basil and tomato dressing, with lots of salad ideas, including the Smoked Haddock Salad, and the Bruschetta with Anchoiade accompanied by a mixed salad of tomatoes and mozzarella cheese.

These delicious pinwheels are perfect for serving with drinks before dinner. If you prefer, use a ready-made anchovy paste, available in tubes in most large supermarkets, to save time.

Anchovy Bites

MAKES 30

1½ cups all-purpose flour, plus extra for dusting
6 tbsp butter, cut into small pieces
4 tbsp freshly grated Parmesan cheese
3 tbsp Dijon mustard
2–3 tbsp cold water
salt and pepper

anchoiade

1¾ oz/50 g canned anchovy fillets in olive oil, drained
scant/½ cup milk
2 garlic cloves, chopped coarsely
1 tbsp coarsely chopped fresh flatleaf parsley
1 tbsp coarsely chopped fresh basil
1 tbsp lemon juice
2 tbsp blanched almonds, toasted and coarsely chopped
4 tbsp olive oil

NUTRITION
Calories 77; Sugars 0.5 g; Protein 2 g; Carbohydrate 5 g; Fat 5 g; Saturates 2 g

 easy

 1 hr

20 mins

1 To make the pie dough, strain the flour into a large bowl. Add the butter and rub it in with your fingertips until the mixture resembles breadcrumbs. Stir in half the Parmesan cheese and salt. Add enough cold water to form a firm dough. Knead briefly, wrap in plastic wrap and let chill in the refrigerator for 30 minutes.

2 Meanwhile, make the anchoiade. Put the drained anchovies into a small bowl and pour over the milk to cover. Let soak for 10 minutes. Drain the anchovies and pat dry on paper towels. Discard the milk.

3 Coarsely chop the anchovies and put into a food processor or blender with the garlic, parsley, basil, lemon juice, almonds and 2 tablespoons of the oil and process until smooth. Transfer to a bowl and stir in the remaining olive oil and pepper to taste.

4 Remove the pie dough from the refrigerator and roll out very thinly on a lightly floured counter to a rectangle measuring 20 x 15 inches/50 x 38 cm. Spread thinly with 2 tablespoons of the anchoiade and the Dijon mustard. Sprinkle over the remaining Parmesan cheese and some pepper.

5 Starting from a long edge, roll up tightly, then slice crossways into ½-inch/1-cm thick slices. Arrange cut-side up and well spaced on a non-stick baking sheet. Cook in a preheated oven, 400°F/200°C, for 20 minutes until golden. Let cool on a wire rack.

This colorful salad is full of flavor and textures. Here mixed cherry tomatoes and beefsteak or plum tomatoes are used, but the salad will work equally well with whatever ripe tomatoes are available.

Bruschetta *with* Anchoiade

1 Slice the mozzarella cheese into thick slices. Set aside. Halve the cherry tomatoes and thickly slice the plum or beefsteak tomatoes.

2 To make the dressing, whisk the olive oil, balsamic vinegar, and seasoning together in a small bowl.

3 Toast the bread on both sides, then rub one side with the garlic clove. Drizzle with a little olive oil. Spread the anchoiade on the toasts.

4 To assemble the salad, arrange the sliced tomatoes on each of 4 serving plates and sprinkle with some of the cherry tomatoes.

5 Top the toasts with the mozzarella slices and 2–3 halved cherry tomatoes. Cook under a preheated medium–hot broiler for 3–4 minutes until softened. Put 2 slices of toast on the plates, then drizzle over the dressing. Sprinkle with basil leaves and pepper and serve at once.

SERVES 4

10½ oz/300 g buffalo mozzarella cheese
1 cup orange cherry tomatoes
1 cup red cherry tomatoes
2 ripe plum or red beefsteak tomatoes
2 ripe orange or yellow beefsteak tomatoes
4 tbsp extra virgin olive oil,
    plus extra for drizzling
1 tbsp balsamic vinegar
8 thick slices ciabatta or
    other rustic country bread
1 garlic clove
4 tbsp anchoiade (see page 20)
handful of fresh basil leaves
salt and pepper

NUTRITION
Calories 583; Sugars 5 g; Protein 28 g;
Carbohydrate 39 g; Fat 35 g; Saturates 12 g

easy

10 mins

4 mins

🍳 COOK'S TIP
Look for Italian mozzarella cheese made from buffalo milk for a real authentic taste of Italy.

Translated literally, Bagna Cauda means "hot bath." This is a typical dish from Piedmont in Italy, where it is always eaten by large groups gathered around the table.

Bagna Cauda *with* Crudités

SERVES 8

1 yellow bell pepper
3 celery stalks
2 carrots
½ cauliflower
½ cup mushrooms
1 fennel bulb
1 bunch of scallions
2 beets, cooked and peeled
8 radishes
8 oz/225 g boiled new potatoes
1 cup olive oil (not extra virgin)
5 garlic cloves, crushed
1¾ oz/50 g canned anchovy fillets in oil, drained and chopped
8 tbsp butter
scallion curls, to garnish

1 Prepare the vegetables. Seed and slice the bell pepper thickly. Cut the celery into 3-inch/7.5-cm lengths. Cut the carrots into batons. Score the tops of the mushrooms. Separate the cauliflower into florets. Cut the fennel in half lengthwise, then cut each half into 4 lengthwise. Trim the scallions. Cut the beets into eighths. Trim the radishes and cut the potatoes in half, if large. Arrange the prepared vegetables on a large serving platter.

2 Heat the olive oil very gently in a pan over low heat. Add the garlic and anchovies and cook very gently, stirring, until the anchovies have dissolved. Take care not to brown or burn the garlic.

3 Add the butter and as soon as it has melted, transfer to a small serving dish. Garnish with a few scallion curls and serve immediately with the selection of prepared crudités.

NUTRITION
Calories *421*; Sugars *6 g*; Protein *7 g*;
Carbohydrate *25 g*; Fat *33 g*; Saturates *11 g*

easy

20–30 mins

5–10 mins

🍴 **COOK'S TIP**

If you have one, a fondue set is perfect for serving this dish as the sauce can be kept hot at the table.

In Spain, giant garlic shrimp are cooked in small half-glazed earthenware dishes called *cazuela*. The shrimp arrive sizzling at your table, with plenty of local bread to mop up the delicious juices.

Giant Garlic Shrimp

1 Heat the olive oil in a large skillet over low heat. Add the garlic and chiles and cook for 1–2 minutes until softened, but not colored.

2 Add the shrimp and stir-fry for 2–3 minutes until heated through and coated in the oil and garlic mixture. Remove the skillet from the heat.

3 Add the parsley and stir well to mix. Season to taste with salt and pepper.

4 Transfer the shrimp and garlic oil to 4 warmed serving dishes and garnish with lemon wedges. Serve at once with lots of crusty bread.

SERVES 4

1 cup olive oil
4 garlic cloves, chopped finely
2 hot fresh red chiles, seeded and finely chopped
1 lb/450 g cooked jumbo shrimp
2 tbsp chopped fresh flatleaf parsley
salt and pepper
lemon wedges, to garnish
crusty bread, to serve

NUTRITION
Calories *385*; Sugars *0 g*; Protein *26 g*; Carbohydrate *1 g*; Fat *31 g*; Saturates *5 g*

 easy

 5 mins

5–8 mins

COOK'S TIP

If using raw shrimp, cook them as above but increase the cooking time to 5–6 minutes so that the shrimp are cooked through and turn bright pink.

These delicious little spring rolls are perfect as part of a selection of canapés. Serve with a selection of dips, as suggested in the recipe.

Mini Shrimp Spring Rolls

SERVES 4

½ cup dried rice vermicelli
1 carrot, cut into short thin sticks
¼ cup snow peas, shredded
   thinly lengthwise
3 scallions, chopped finely
3½ oz/100 g cooked peeled shrimp
2 garlic cloves, crushed
1 tsp sesame oil
2 tbsp light soy sauce
1 tsp chili sauce
7 oz/200 g phyllo pastry, cut into
   6-inch/15-cm squares
1 egg white, beaten
2 cups vegetable oil, for deep-frying
dark soy sauce, sweet chili sauce, or peanut
   sauce (see page 25),
   for dipping

NUTRITION
Calories 355; Sugars 3 g; Protein 13 g;
Carbohydrate 44 g; Fat 14 g; Saturates 2 g

easy

10 mins

20 mins

1 Cook the rice vermicelli according to the package instructions. Drain thoroughly. Coarsely chop and set aside. Bring a pan of salted water to a boil over medium heat. Add the carrot and snow peas and blanch for 1 minute. Drain and refresh under cold running water. Drain again and pat dry on paper towels. Mix with the noodles and add the scallions, shrimp, garlic, sesame oil, soy sauce, and chile sauce. Set aside.

2 Fold the phyllo pastry squares in half diagonally to form triangles. Lay a triangle on the counter, with the fold facing you, and place a spoonful of the mixture in the center. Roll over the wrapper to enclose the filling, then bring over the corners to enclose the ends of the roll. Brush the point of the spring roll furthest from you with a little beaten egg white and continue rolling to seal. Continue with the remaining phyllo triangles and mixture to make about 30 spring rolls.

3 Fill a deep-fat fryer or deep pan about one-third full with vegetable oil and heat to 375°F/190°C, or until a cube of bread browns in 30 seconds. Add the spring rolls, 4 or 5 at a time, and deep-fry for 1–2 minutes or until golden and crisp. Drain on paper towels. Keep warm while you cook the remaining spring rolls.

4 Serve the spring rolls with dark soy sauce, sweet chili sauce, or peanut sauce for dipping.

It is well worth seeking a supplier of Thai ingredients, such as lemongrass and lime leaves, as they add such distinctive flavors for which there are no real substitutes.

Shrimp Satay

1 Slit the shrimp down their backs and remove the black vein, if any. Set aside. Mix the marinade ingredients together and add the shrimp. Mix well, cover and set aside in the refrigerator for at least 8 hours or overnight.

2 To make the peanut sauce, finely chop most of the peanuts, leaving a few whole. Then heat the vegetable oil in a large skillet until very hot. Add the garlic and cook until just starting to color. Add the red curry paste and mix well, cooking for another 30 seconds. Add the coconut milk, stock, sugar, salt, and lemon juice and stir well. Boil for 1–2 minutes, stirring constantly. Add the chopped peanuts and bread crumbs, mixing well. Pour the sauce into a bowl and set aside.

3 Using 4 metal skewers, thread 3 shrimp on to each. Cook under a preheated hot broiler or transfer to a lit barbecue and cook over hot coals for about 3–4 minutes on each side until just cooked through. Transfer the shrimp to a large serving plate and garnish with lime wedges. Serve immediately with the peanut sauce, garnished a lime wedge and a few whole peanuts.

SERVES 4

12 raw jumbo shrimp, peeled
lime wedges, to garnish
marinade
1 tsp ground coriander
1 tsp ground cumin
2 tbsp light soy sauce
4 tbsp vegetable oil
1 tbsp curry powder
1 tbsp ground turmeric
½ cup coconut milk
3 tbsp sugar
peanut sauce
2 tbsp vegetable oil
3 garlic cloves, crushed
1 tbsp red curry paste (see page 74)
½ cup coconut milk
1 cup fish or chicken bouillon
1 tbsp sugar
1 tsp salt
1 tbsp lemon juice
4 tbsp unsalted peanuts,
4 tbsp dried bread crumbs

NUTRITION
Calories 367; Sugars 25 g; Protein 9 g; Carbohydrate 33 g; Fat 23 g; Saturates 3 q

easy

8 hrs

7–10 mins

COOK'S TIP

Leave the tails intact on the shrimps before cooking. This makes them easier to hold when eating.

These little fish cakes are very popular as street food in Thailand and also make a perfect appetizer with a spicy peanut dip.

Thai Fish Cakes

SERVES 4

12 oz/350 g white fish fillet, such as cod or
    haddock, skinned
1 tbsp Thai fish sauce
2 tsp Thai red curry paste
1 tbsp lime juice
1 garlic clove, crushed
4 dried kaffir lime leaves, crumbled
1 egg white
3 tbsp chopped fresh cilantro
¼ cup vegetable oil, for pan-frying
salad greens, to serve

peanut dip
1 small, fresh red chile
1 tbsp light soy sauce
1 tbsp lime juice
1 tbsp light brown sugar
3 tbsp chunky peanut butter
4 tbsp coconut milk
salt and pepper
chopped fresh chives, to garnish

NUTRITION
Calories *205 g*; Sugars *6 g*; Protein *17 g*;
Carbohydrate *7 g*; Fat *12 g*; Saturates *2 g*

easy

15 mins

15 mins

1 Put the fish fillet into a food processor with the Thai fish sauce, red curry paste, lime juice, garlic, lime leaves, and egg white and process until a smooth paste forms.

2 Add the chopped cilantro and quickly process again until mixed. Divide the mixture into 8–10 pieces and roll into balls between the palms of your hands, then flatten to make small round patties and set aside.

3 To make the dip, halve and seed the chile, then chop finely. Place in a small pan with the soy sauce, lime juice, sugar, peanut butter, and coconut milk and heat gently, stirring constantly, until thoroughly blended. Adjust the seasoning, adding more lime juice or sugar to taste. Transfer to a small bowl, garnish with chopped chives and set aside.

4 Heat the vegetable oil in a skillet over medium heat. Add the fish cakes, in batches, and cook for 3–4 minutes on each side until golden-brown. Drain on paper towels and serve them hot on a bed of salad greens with the chile-flavored peanut dip.

These pretty little steamed and fried crab cakes are usually served as a snack, but they also make an appetizing starter.

Steamed Crab Cakes

1 Line 8 x ½-cup ramekins or foil containers with the banana leaves, cutting them to shape.

2 Mix the garlic, lemongrass, pepper, and cilantro together. Mash the creamed coconut with the lime juice until smooth. Stir it into the other ingredients with the crabmeat and Thai fish sauce.

3 Whisk the egg whites in a clean, dry bowl until stiff, then lightly and evenly fold them into the crab mixture. Spoon the mixture into the prepared ramekins or foil containers and press down lightly. Brush the tops with egg yolk and top each with a cilantro leaf.

4 Place in a steamer half-filled with boiling water, then cover with a close-fitting lid and steam for 15 minutes or until firm to the touch. Pour off the excess liquid and remove from the ramekins or foil containers.

5 Fill a deep pan one-third full with corn oil and heat to 350°F/180°C, or until a cube of bread browns in 30 seconds. Add the crab cakes and deep-fry for 1 minute, turning them over once, until golden brown. Put the chili sauce into a bowl and garnish with cilantro. Transfer the crab cakes to a serving plate and serve hot with chili sauce.

SERVES 4

1–2 banana leaves
2 garlic cloves, crushed
1 tsp finely chopped lemongrass
½ tsp pepper
2 tbsp chopped fresh cilantro, plus extra to garnish
3 tbsp creamed coconut
1 tbsp lime juice
7 oz/200 g cooked crabmeat, flaked
1 tbsp Thai fish sauce
2 egg whites
1 egg yolk, beaten lightly
8 fresh cilantro leaves
2 cups corn oil, for deep-frying
chili sauce, to serve

NUTRITION
Calories *156*; Sugars *1 g*; Protein *13 g*;
Carbohydrate *2 g*; Fat *11 g*; Saturates *4 g*

  easy

25 mins

 20 mins

COOK'S TIP

For best results, always whisk egg whites in a spotlessly clean, dry bowl, which is free from grease, otherwise they will not hold their shape very well.

These crisp, golden-fried little mouthfuls are packed with flavor and served with a hot-and-sweet soy dip—perfect to stimulate appetites at the start of a meal, or as a tasty snack.

Jumbo Shrimp Rolls

S E R V E S 4

dip
1 small red bird's-eye chile, seeded
1 tsp honey
4 tbsp soy sauce

rolls
2 tbsp fresh cilantro leaves
1 garlic clove
1½ tsp Thai red curry paste
16 wonton wrappers
1 egg white, beaten lightly
16 raw jumbo shrimp, peeled
    with tails intact
2 cups corn oil, for deep-frying
whole fresh red chiles, to garnish

N U T R I T I O N
Calories *175*; Sugars *2 g*; Protein *10 g*;
Carbohydrate *7 g*; Fat *12 g*; Saturates *1 g*

     easy
     10 mins
              20 mins

1 To make the dip, finely chop the chile, then mix with the honey and soy and stir well. Set aside until required.

2 To make the prawn rolls, finely chop the cilantro and garlic, and mix with the red curry paste.

3 Brush each wonton wrapper with egg white and place a small dab of the cilantro mixture in the center. Place a shrimp on top.

4 Fold the wonton wrapper over, enclosing the shrimp and leaving the tail exposed. Repeat with the other shrimp.

5 Fill a deep saucepan one-third full with corn oil and heat to 350°F/180°C, or until a cube of bread turns brown in 30 seconds. Add the shrimp rolls in small batches and deep-fry for 1–2 minutes each until golden-brown and crisp. Drain on paper towels and transfer them to a large serving plate. Garnish with fresh chiles and serve with the chile dip. Give each guest a small bowl filled with hot water and a lemon slice so that they can wash their fingers afterward.

C O O K ' S T I P

If you prefer, replace the wonton wrappers with phyllo pastry—use a long strip of dough, place the paste and a shrimp on one end, brush with egg white and wrap the dough around the shrimp to enclose and deep-fry.

A popular delicacy found throughout many countries in the East, these crisp, golden-fried toasts are very simple to make and perfect to serve with drinks at parties.

Shrimp *and* Chicken Sesame Toasts

1 Place the chicken and shrimp in a food processor and process until very finely chopped. Add the egg, scallions, garlic, cilantro, Thai fish sauce, pepper, and salt, and pulse for a few seconds to mix well. Transfer to a bowl.

2 Spread the mixture evenly over the slices of bread, right to the edges. Sprinkle the sesame seeds over a plate and press the spread side of each slice of bread into them to coat evenly.

3 Using a sharp knife, cut the bread into small rectangles, making 6 per slice.

4 Heat a ½-inch/1-cm depth of corn oil in a wide skillet until very hot. Add the bread rectangles, in batches, and cook quickly for 2–3 minutes until golden-brown, turning them over once.

5 Drain the toasts well on paper towels, transfer to a large serving dish and garnish with thinly shredded scallion curls. Serve immediately.

SERVES 4

4 boneless, skinless chicken thighs
3½ oz/100 g cooked peeled shrimp
1 small egg, beaten
3 scallions, chopped finely
2 garlic cloves, crushed
2 tbsp fresh cilantro, chopped
1 tbsp Thai fish sauce
½ tsp pepper
¼ tsp salt
12 slices white bread, crusts removed
8 tbsp sesame seeds
½ cup corn oil, for pan-frying
shredded scallion curls, to garnish

NUTRITION
Calories *491*; Sugars *3 g*; Protein *25 g*; Carbohydrate *39 g*; Fat *27 g*; Saturates *4 g*

 ✪✪   easy

🕙   10 mins

    20 mins

🧑‍🍳 COOK'S TIP

If you're catering for a party, make the toasts in advance. Chill for up to 3 days or place in a sealed container and freeze for up to 1 month. Thaw overnight in the refrigerator, then cook in a hot oven for 5 minutes to reheat thoroughly.

These little pots of shrimp in spicy butter are a classic English dish, originating from Morecambe Bay in Lancashire, where they are still made today.

Potted Shrimp

SERVES 4

1¼ cups unsalted butter
14 oz/400 g brown shrimp in their shells or 8 oz/225 g cooked peeled shrimp
pinch of cayenne pepper
½ tsp ground mace
1 garlic clove, crushed
1 tbsp chopped fresh parsley
salt and pepper
brown bread, to serve

to garnish
lemon wedges
fresh parsley sprigs
whole cooked shrimp

1 Heat the butter in a small pan over low heat until melted and foaming. Set aside for 10 minutes or until the butter separates. Carefully skim off the clear yellow liquid and discard the white milk solids. The clear yellow oil remaining is clarified butter.

2 Peel the shrimp, discarding the shells. Heat 2 tablespoons of the clarified butter in a skillet over low heat. Add the shrimp and stir in the cayenne, mace, and garlic. Increase the heat and stir-fry for 30 seconds until very hot. Remove the skillet from the heat, stir in the parsley and season to taste with salt and pepper.

3 Divide the shrimp among 4 small ramekins, pressing down with the back of a spoon. Pour over the remaining clarified butter to cover. Let chill in the refrigerator until the butter has set.

4 Remove the ramekins from the refrigerator 30 minutes before serving to let the butter soften. Toast the brown bread and transfer to a serving plate. Garnish the shrimp with lemon wedges, fresh parsley, and whole shrimp, then serve with the toast.

NUTRITION

Calories *487*; Sugars *0 g*; Protein *14 g*; Carbohydrate *0.5 g*; Fat *48 g*; Saturates *31 g*

 easy

1 hr 30 mins

 12 mins

COOK'S TIP

The most authentic shrimp to use for this recipe are the tiny brown ones. They have a full flavor and soak up the butter well. If your fish market can't supply them, substitute the pink peeled variety.

This is a variation on the classic "Devils on Horseback"—oysters wrapped in bacon. This version uses freshly steamed mussels, stuffed inside marinated prunes, which are then wrapped in smoky bacon and broiled with a sticky-sweet glaze.

Prunes Stuffed *with* Mussels

1 Mix the port, honey and garlic together, then season to taste with salt and pepper. Put the prunes into a small bowl and pour over the port mixture. Cover and let marinate for at least 4 hours or preferably overnight.

2 Next day, clean the mussels by scrubbing or scraping the shells and pulling out any beards that are attached to them. Put the mussels into a large pan with just the water that clings to their shells and cook, covered, over high heat for 3–4 minutes until all the mussels have opened. Discard any mussels that remain closed.

3 Strain the mussels, reserving the cooking liquid. Let cool, then remove the mussels from their shells.

4 Using the back of a knife, stretch the bacon slices, then cut in half widthwise. Lift the prunes from their marinade, reserving any that remains.

5 Stuff each prune with a mussel, then wrap with a piece of bacon. Secure with a toothpick. Repeat to make 24.

6 Simmer the mussel cooking liquid and remaining marinade together in a pan until reduced and syrupy. Brush the stuffed prunes with this mixture. Place under a preheated hot broiler and cook for 3–4 minutes on each side, turning regularly and brushing with the marinade, until the bacon is crisp and golden. Serve while still hot, with salad greens.

SERVES 4

3 tbsp port
1 tbsp honey
2 garlic cloves, crushed
24 large stoned prunes
24 live mussels
12 bacon slices
salt and pepper
salad greens, to serve

NUTRITION
Calories *184*; Sugars *31 g*; Protein *9 g*;
Carbohydrate *33 g*; Fat *1 g*; Saturates *0.5 g*

 easy

4 hrs 30 mins

10–15 mins

If you find making mayonnaise difficult, or if you don't like to eat raw eggs, use a good-quality ready-made mayonnaise and mix in the garlic and mixed herbs.

Mussel Fritters

SERVES 4 – 6

1½ cups all-purpose flour
pinch of salt
1 egg
1 cup lager of your choice
2 lb/900 g live mussels
2 cups vegetable oil, for deep-frying

garlic and herb mayonnaise
1 egg yolk
1 tsp Dijon mustard
1 tsp white wine vinegar
2 garlic cloves, crushed
2 tbsp chopped fresh mixed herbs, such as parsley, chives, basil, and thyme
1 cup olive oil
salt and pepper

to garnish
lemon slices
fresh parsley sprigs

NUTRITION
Calories 771; Sugars 2 g; Protein 16 g;
Carbohydrate 37 g; Fat 61 g; Saturates 9 g

⭐⭐   easy

🕐   40 mins

🕐   12 mins

1 To make the batter, put the flour into the bowl with the salt. Add the egg and half the lager and whisk until smooth. Gradually add the remaining lager, whisking until smooth. Set aside for 30 minutes.

2 Clean the mussels by scrubbing or scraping the shells and pulling out any beards that are attached to them. Discard any with broken shells or any that refuse to close when tapped. Put the mussels into a large pan with just the water that clings to their shells and cook, covered, over high heat for about 3–4 minutes, shaking the pan occasionally, until all the mussels have opened. Discard any mussels that remain closed. Drain and set aside until cool enough to handle, then remove the mussels from their shells.

3 To make the mayonnaise, put the egg yolk, mustard, vinegar, garlic, herbs, and seasoning into a food processor or blender and process until frothy. Keeping the machine running, gradually add the olive oil, drop by drop to start with, until the mixture starts to thicken. Continue adding the olive oil in a steady stream until all the oil is incorporated. Season to taste with salt and pepper and add a little hot water if the mixture seems too thick. Set aside.

4 Meanwhile, fill a deep pan about one-third full with vegetable oil and heat to 375°F/190°C, or until a cube of bread browns in 30 seconds. Drop the mussels, a few at a time, into the batter and lift out with a draining spoon. Drop into the oil and cook for 1–2 minutes until the batter is crisp and golden. Drain on paper towels. Transfer the fritters to warmed serving plates, garnish with lemon slices and parsley, then serve hot with the mayonnaise.

These delicious morsels make an impressive, yet quick appetizer. Serve them with some crusty bread to mop up any juices.

Mussels *with* Pesto

1 Clean the mussels by scrubbing or scraping the shells and pulling out any beards that are attached to them. Discard any with broken shells or any that refuse to close when tapped. Put the mussels into a large pan with just the water on their shells and cook, covered, over high heat for 3–4 minutes, shaking the pan occasionally, until all the mussels have opened. Discard any mussels that remain closed. Strain, reserving the cooking liquid, and set aside until cool enough to handle.

2 Strain the cooking liquid into a clean pan and simmer until reduced to about 1 tablespoon. Put the liquid into a food processor with the basil, garlic, pine nuts, and Parmesan cheese and process until finely chopped. Add the olive oil and bread crumbs and process until well mixed.

3 Open the mussels and loosen from their shells, discarding the empty half of the shell. Divide the pesto bread crumbs among the mussels.

4 Cook under a preheated hot broiler until the bread crumbs are crisp and golden, and the mussels heated through. Transfer to a large, warmed serving plate, garnish with tomato slices and basil leaves and serve immediately.

SERVES 4

2 lb/900 g live mussels
6 tbsp chopped fresh basil
2 garlic cloves, crushed
1 tbsp pine nuts, toasted
2 tbsp freshly grated Parmesan cheese
scant ½ cup olive oil
2 cups fresh white bread crumbs
salt and pepper

to garnish
tomato slices
fresh basil leaves

NUTRITION
Calories *399*; Sugars *1 g*; Protein *14 g*; Carbohydrate *17 g*; Fat *31 g*; Saturates *5 g*

easy

20 mins

12 mins

🍳 **COOK'S TIP**

If you want an alternative to pine nuts add 3 oz/85 g coarsely chopped, drained sun-dried tomatoes in oil to the pesto instead.

These small toasts are easy to prepare and are one of the most popular Chinese appetizers in the West. Make sure you serve plenty of them as they are very tasty!

Shrimp *and* Sesame Triangles

SERVES 4

8 oz/225 g cooked, peeled shrimp
1 scallion
¼ tsp salt
1 tsp light soy sauce
1 tbsp cornstarch
1 egg white, beaten
3 thin slices white bread, crusts removed
4 tbsp sesame seeds
2 cups vegetable oil, for deep-frying

1 Put the shrimp and scallion into a food processor and process until finely minced. Alternatively, chop them very finely. Transfer to a bowl and stir in the salt, soy sauce, cornstarch, and egg white.

2 Spread the mixture onto one side of each slice of bread. Spread the sesame seeds on top of the mixture, pressing down well.

3 Cut each slice into 4 equal triangles or strips.

4 Heat the vegetable oil for deep-frying in a preheated wok over medium–high heat until almost smoking. Carefully place the triangles in the oil, coated side down, and cook for 2–3 minutes until golden brown. Remove with a draining spoon and drain on paper towels. Serve immediately.

NUTRITION
Calories 237; Sugars 1 g; Protein 18 g;
Carbohydrate 15 g; Fat 12 g; Saturates 2 g

easy

5 mins

10 mins

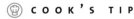 **COOK'S TIP**

You could add ½ teaspoon very finely chopped fresh gingerroot and 1 teaspoon Chinese rice wine to the prawn mixture at the end of Step 1, if desired.

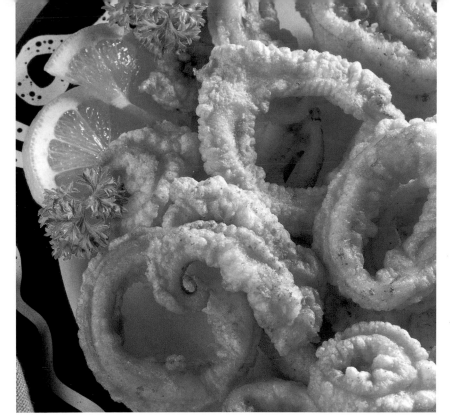

The batter may not be traditional, but this is a perfect dish to serve as part of a selection of tapas, or little dishes, with drinks as they do in Spain.

Calamari

1 Strain the flour and salt together into a bowl. Add the eggs and half the soda water and whisk together until smooth. Gradually whisk in the remaining soda water until the batter is smooth. Set aside.

2 To prepare the whole squid, hold the body firmly and grasp the tentacles just inside the body. Pull firmly to remove the innards. Find the transparent "backbone" and remove. Grasp the wings on the outside of the body and pull to remove the outer skin. Trim the tentacles just below the beak and set aside.

3 Wash the body and tentacles under cold running water. Slice the body across into ½-inch/1-cm rings. Drain well on paper towels.

4 Meanwhile, fill a deep pan about one-third full with vegetable oil and heat to 375°F/190°C, or until a cube of bread browns in 30 seconds.

5 Dip the squid rings and tentacles into the batter, a few at a time, and drop into the hot oil. Deep-fry for 1–2 minutes until crisp and golden. Drain on paper towels. Keep warm while you cook the remaining squid. Transfer the squid to a large serving plate, garnish with lemon wedges and parsley sprigs and serve immediately.

SERVES 4

1 cup all-purpose flour
1 tsp salt
2 eggs
¾ cup soda water
1 lb/450 g prepared squid (see cook's tip), cut into rings
2 cups vegetable oil, for deep-frying

to garnish
lemon wedges
fresh parsley sprigs

NUTRITION
Calories 333; Sugars 0.5 g; Protein 24 g; Carbohydrate 24 g; Fat 17 g; Saturates 2 g

   easy
10 mins
10 mins

🍳 COOK'S TIP

If you don't like the idea of cleaning squid yourself, get your fishmonger to do it. Sometimes, squid is even sold already cut into rings. Alternatively, you could use prepared baby squid for this dish.

This is a very typical Greek recipe for stuffing squid. Most large supermarkets with fish counters sell baby squid already cleaned.

Stuffed Squid

SERVES 4

12 baby squid, cleaned
1 tsp salt
4 tbsp olive oil
1 small onion, chopped finely
1 garlic clove, chopped finely
1 cup basmati rice
1 tbsp seedless raisins
1 tbsp pine nuts, toasted
1 tbsp chopped fresh flatleaf parsley
14 oz/400 g canned chopped tomatoes
¼ cup sun-dried tomatoes in oil, drained
   and finely chopped
½ cup dry white wine
salt and pepper
lemon slices, to garnish
crusty bread, to serve

1 Separate the tentacles from the body of the squid. Chop the tentacles and set aside. Rub the squid tubes inside and out with the salt and set aside while you prepare the stuffing.

2 Heat 1 tablespoon of the olive oil in a skillet over low heat. Add the onion and garlic and cook for 4–5 minutes until softened and lightly browned. Add the chopped tentacles and cook for 2–3 minutes. Add the rice, raisins, pine nuts, and parsley, then season to taste with salt and pepper. Remove from the heat.

3 Let the rice mixture cool slightly, then spoon it into the squid tubes, about three-quarters full to let the rice expand. You may need to open the squid tubes a little by making a small cut. Secure each squid with a toothpick.

4 Heat the remaining oil in a large ovenproof casserole over medium heat. Add the squid and cook for a few minutes on all sides until lightly browned. Add the tomatoes, sun-dried tomatoes, wine and seasoning to taste. Bake in a preheated oven, 350°F/180°C, for 45 minutes. Transfer to a large serving plate, garnish with lemon slices and serve with crusty bread.

NUTRITION
Calories 300; Sugars 9 g; Protein 12 g;
Carbohydrate 19 g; Fat 18 g; Saturates 2 g

moderate

25 mins

1 hr

 COOK'S TIP

If you have difficulty finding baby squid, larger ones work very well and the cooking time is the same. Use cleaned squid weighing 8 oz/225 g in total for the amount of stuffing in this recipe.

Tempura is a classic Japanese batter made with egg, flour, and water. The batter mix is very cold and very lumpy, which gives the dish its characteristic appearance. It should be eaten straight away.

Tempura Smelt

1 To make the mayonnaise, put the egg yolk, lime juice, chile, cilantro, and seasoning into a food processor and mix until foaming. Keeping the machine running, gradually add the olive oil, drop by drop to start with, until the mixture starts to thicken. Continue adding the olive oil in a steady stream until all the oil is incorporated. Season to taste with salt and pepper and add a little hot water if the mixture seems too thick. Set aside.

2 To make the tempura smelt, wash the fish under cold running water and pat dry with paper towels. Set aside. Strain the flour, cornstarch, and salt together into a large bowl. Whisk the water, egg, and ice cubes together and pour onto the flour. Whisk briefly until the mixture is runny, but still lumpy with dry bits of flour still apparent.

3 Meanwhile, fill a deep pan about one-third full with vegetable oil and heat to 375°F/190°C, or until a cube of bread browns in 30 seconds.

4 Dip the smelt, a few at a time, into the batter and carefully drop into the hot oil. Deep-fry for 1 minute until the batter is crisp, but not browned. Drain on paper towels. Keep warm while you cook the remaining smelt. Serve hot with the chile and lime mayonnaise.

SERVES 4

1 lb/450 g smelt, thawed if frozen
¾ cup all-purpose flour
⅓ cup cornstarch
½ tsp salt
1 cup cold water
1 egg
a few ice cubes
2 cups vegetable oil, for deep frying

chile and lime mayonnaise

1 egg yolk
1 tbsp lime juice
1 fresh red chile, seeded and finely chopped
2 tbsp chopped fresh cilantro
1 cup light olive oil
salt and pepper

NUTRITION
Calories *790*; Sugars *0.5 g*; Protein *23 g*;
Carbohydrate *31 g*; Fat *64 g*; Saturates *16 q*

 easy

30 mins

 10 mins

This is a quick and easy pâté with plenty of flavor. It originates from Goa, on the west coast of India, an area very famous for its seafood.

Smoked Mackerel Pâté

SERVES 4

7 oz/200 g smoked mackerel fillet
1 small, hot fresh green chile,
    seeded and chopped
1 garlic clove, chopped
3 tbsp fresh cilantro leaves
²/₃ cup sour cream
1 small red onion, chopped finely
2 tbsp lime juice
4 slices white bread, crusts removed
salt and pepper

to garnish
fresh dill sprigs
orange slices
lemon slices

1 Skin and flake the mackerel fillet, removing any small bones. Put the flesh into a food processor along with the chile, garlic, cilantro, and sour cream. Process until smooth.

2 Transfer the mixture to a bowl and mix in the onion and lime juice. Season to taste with salt and pepper. The pâté will seem very soft at this stage, but will firm up in the refrigerator. Let chill in the refrigerator for several hours or overnight if possible.

3 To make the Melba toasts, place the trimmed bread slices under a preheated medium–hot broiler and toast lightly on both sides. Split the toasts in half horizontally, then cut each across diagonally to form 4 triangles per slice.

4 Put the triangles, untoasted side up, under the preheated broiler and toast until golden and curled at the edges. To serve, arrange the smoked mackerel pâté on a serving plate and garnish with a few sprigs of fresh dill, orange, and lemon slices and the Melba toast.

NUTRITION
Calories *316*; Sugars *3 g*; Protein *13 g*;
Carbohydrate *14 g*; Fat *23 g*; Saturates *8 g*

 easy

4 hrs 30 mins

5 mins

 **COOK'S TIP**

This pâté is also very good served with crudités.

Smoked haddock goes well with eggs. Here it is teamed with hard-boiled quail's eggs and topped with a delicious creamy chive dressing.

Smoked Haddock Salad

1 Fill a large skillet with water and bring to a boil over medium heat. Add the smoked haddock fillet, cover and remove from the heat. Leave for 10 minutes until the fish is tender. Lift from the poaching water, drain and leave until cool enough to handle. Flake the flesh, removing any small bones. Set aside. Discard the poaching water.

2 Whisk the olive oil, lemon juice, sour cream, hot water, chives and seasoning together. Stir in the tomato. Set aside.

3 Bring a small pan of water to a boil over medium heat. Carefully lower the quail's eggs into the water. Cook the eggs for 3–4 minutes from when the water returns to a boil (3 minutes for a slightly soft center, 4 minutes for a firm center). Drain immediately and refresh under cold running water. Carefully peel the eggs, cut in half lengthwise and set aside.

4 Toast the bread and cut each across diagonally to form 4 triangles. Arrange 2 halves on each of 4 serving plates. Top with the salad greens, then the flaked fish and finally the quail's eggs. Spoon over the dressing and garnish with a few sprigs of fresh parsley, lime slices, and tomato halves.

SERVES 4

12 oz/350 g smoked haddock fillet
4 tbsp olive oil
1 tbsp lemon juice
2 tbsp sour cream
1 tbsp hot water
2 tbsp chopped fresh chives
1 plum tomato, peeled, seeded, and diced
8 quail's eggs
4 thick slices multigrain bread
4 oz/115 g mixed salad greens
salt and pepper

to garnish
fresh flatleaf parsley sprigs
lime slices
tomatoes, halved

NUTRITION
Calories 223; Sugars 23 g; Protein 21 g; Carbohydrate 25 g; Fat 4 g; Saturates 1 g

  easy

🕐 15 mins

🕐 10 mins

🍳 COOK'S TIP

When buying smoked haddock, and smoked fish in general, look for undyed fish, which is always superior in quality.

If you can find them, use small chiles, called bird's-eye, for the dipping sauce. They are extremely hot however, so remove the seeds, if you prefer.

Thai Fish Cakes *with* Dipping Sauce

SERVES 4

1 lb/450 g firm white fish, such as hake, haddock, or cod, skinned and coarsely chopped
1 tbsp Thai fish sauce
1 tbsp red curry paste (see page 74)
1 kaffir lime leaf, shredded finely
2 tbsp chopped fresh cilantro
1 egg
1 tsp brown sugar
large pinch of salt
1½ oz/40 g green beans, sliced thinly crossways
¼ cup vegetable oil, for pan-frying

dipping sauce

4 tbsp sugar
1 tbsp cold water
3 tbsp white rice vinegar
2 small, fresh hot chiles, chopped finely
1 tbsp Thai fish sauce

to garnish

scallion tassels
fresh chile flowers

NUTRITION

Calories 223; Sugars 23 g; Protein 21 g; Carbohydrate 25 g; Fat 4 g; Saturates 1 g

easy

15 mins

10 mins

1 To make the fish cakes, put the fish, Thai fish sauce, red curry paste, lime leaf, cilantro, egg, sugar, and salt into a food processor and process until smooth. Transfer to a bowl and stir in the green beans. Set aside.

2 To make the dipping sauce, put the sugar, water, and rice vinegar into a small pan and heat gently until the sugar has dissolved. Bring to a boil and let simmer for 2 minutes. Remove from the heat and stir in the chiles and Thai fish sauce and let cool.

3 Heat a skillet with enough vegetable oil to generously cover the bottom of the skillet. Divide the fish mixture into 16 little balls. Flatten the balls into patties and cook in the hot oil for 1–2 minutes on each side until golden. Drain on paper towels. Transfer to a large serving platter, garnish with scallion tassels and chile flowers and serve hot with the dipping sauce.

COOK'S TIP

It isn't necessary to use the most expensive white fish in this recipe as the other flavors are very strong. Use whatever is cheapest.

These crab cakes contain a high proportion of crabmeat and are therefore very light. You can serve them with a warm basil and tomato dressing but they are also delicious with good-quality mayonnaise.

Maryland Crab Cakes

1 Bring a large pan of lightly salted water to a boil over medium heat. Add the potatoes and cook for 15–20 minutes until tender. Drain well and mash with a fork.

2 Mix the crabmeat, scallions, chile, and mayonnaise together in a large bowl. Add the mashed potato, and salt and pepper to taste and mix well. Shape the mixture into 8 cakes.

3 Put the flour, egg, and bread crumbs into separate bowls. Dip the cakes first into the flour, then the egg and finally the bread crumbs to coat. Let chill in the refrigerator for 30 minutes.

4 Heat a skillet with enough vegetable oil to generously cover the bottom of the skillet. Add the cakes, in batches if necessary, and cook for 3–4 minutes on each side until golden and crisp. Drain on paper towels and keep warm while you cook the remaining cakes.

5 Meanwhile, to make the dressing, put the oil, lemon juice, and tomato in a small pan and heat gently over low heat for 2–3 minutes. Remove from the heat and stir in the basil and salt and pepper to taste.

6 Divide the fish cakes between 4 serving plates. Spoon over the dressing and garnish with lemon slices and a few sprigs of fresh dill. Serve immediately.

SERVES 4

8 oz/225 g potatoes, peeled and cut into chunks
2 cups cooked white crabmeat, thawed if frozen
6 scallions, chopped finely
1 small, fresh red chile, seeded and finely chopped
3 tbsp mayonnaise
2 tbsp all-purpose flour
1 egg, beaten lightly
1 cup fresh white bread crumbs
¼ cup vegetable oil, for pan-frying
salt and pepper

dressing
5 tbsp olive oil
1 tbsp lemon juice
1 large ripe tomato, peeled, seeded, and diced
3 tbsp chopped fresh basil

to garnish
lemon slices
fresh dill sprigs

NUTRITION
Calories 549; Sugars 3 g; Protein 29 g; Carbohydrate 34 g; Fat 34 g; Saturates 5 g

 easy

15 mins

30 mins

It is very important to use fresh salmon for this dish. The salt and sugar draw the moisture from the fish, leaving it raw but cured and full of flavor.

Lime *and* Basil Cured Salmon

SERVES 4

2 lb/900 g very fresh salmon fillet, from the head end, skinned
¼ cup sugar
¼ cup sea salt
5 tbsp chopped fresh basil
finely grated rind of 2 limes
1 tsp white peppercorns, crushed lightly
5½ oz/150 g mixed salad greens, to serve

dressing
¾ cup rice vinegar
5 tbsp sugar
finely grated rind of 1 lime
½ tsp English mustard
3 tbsp chopped fresh basil
1 tbsp Japanese pickled ginger, finely shredded

to garnish
handful of fresh chives
cucumber slices

NUTRITION
Calories *382*; Sugars *27 g*; Protein *31 g*; Carbohydrate *27 g*; Fat *17 g*; Saturates *3 g*

 easy
 24 hrs
8 mins

1 Remove any small bones that remain in the salmon fillet. Wash the fish under cold running water and pat dry with paper towels. Place the salmon in a large, non-metallic dish and sprinkle evenly with the sugar, sea salt, basil, lime rind, and peppercorns. Cover and let chill in the refrigerator for 24–48 hours, turning the fish occasionally.

2 To make the dressing, put the rice vinegar and sugar into a small pan and stir gently over low heat until the sugar has dissolved. Then, bring to a boil and let simmer for 5–6 minutes until the liquid is reduced by about one-third. Remove the pan from the heat and stir in the lime rind and mustard. Set aside.

3 Remove the salmon fillet from the marinade, wiping off any excess with paper towels. Slice very thinly.

4 To serve, stir the chopped basil and pickled ginger into the dressing. Toss the salad greens with a little of the dressing and arrange on 6 serving plates. Divide the salmon slices between the plates and drizzle a little dressing over. Garnish with a few chives and serve.

Hot-smoked salmon is increasingly available and is such a treat. Unlike traditional smoked salmon, the fish is smoked in a hot environment so that the flesh cooks conventionally but has a wonderful smoky flavor. This fish is juicy and tender.

Hot-Smoked Salmon Scramble

1 Melt the butter in a large skillet over low heat and when it starts to foam, add the eggs. Leave for a moment to start to set and slowly stir and move the set egg away from the bottom of the skillet to let the uncooked egg take its place. Leave again for a moment and repeat.

2 Before all the egg has set, stir in the heavy cream, flaked salmon, and chopped herbs. Stir to incorporate. Do not overcook the eggs.

3 Meanwhile, toast the split muffins on both sides. Spread with more butter, if desired. Place 2 muffin halves on each of 4 serving plates.

4 When the eggs are cooked, divide among the muffins. Season to taste with salt and pepper and garnish with a few sprigs of fresh parsley and orange wedges. Serve while still warm.

SERVES 4

¼ cup butter
8 eggs, beaten lightly
4 tbsp heavy cream
8 oz/225 g skinless, boneless hot-smoked salmon, flaked
2 tbsp chopped fresh mixed herbs such as chives, basil, and parsley
4 English muffins, split
1–2 tbsp extra butter, for spreading
salt and pepper

to garnish
fresh flatleaf parsley sprigs
orange wedges

NUTRITION
Calories *679*; Sugars *3 g*; Protein *37 g*; Carbohydrate *35 g*; Fat *45 g*; Saturates *20 g*

 moderate
 10–15 mins
30 mins

 COOK'S TIP

If you have difficulty finding hot-smoked salmon, you could use conventional smoked salmon, chopped, instead.

It is best to buy packages of smoked salmon strips for this recipe as they lend themselves to folding more easily than freshly sliced salmon.

Griddled Smoked Salmon

SERVES 4

12 oz/350 g sliced smoked salmon
1 tsp Dijon mustard
1 garlic clove, crushed
2 tsp chopped fresh dill
2 tsp sherry vinegar
4 tbsp olive oil
4 oz/115 g mixed salad greens
salt and pepper

to garnish
fresh dill sprigs
mixed lemon, lime, and orange slices

1 Fold the slices of smoked salmon, making 2 folds accordion-style, so that they form little parcels.

2 To make the vinaigrette, whisk the mustard, garlic, dill, vinegar, and seasoning together in a small bowl. Gradually whisk in the olive oil to form a light emulsion.

3 Heat a ridged griddle until smoking over medium heat. Add the salmon bundles and cook on one side only for 2–3 minutes until heated through and marked from the pan.

4 Meanwhile, dress the salad greens with some of the vinaigrette and divide among 4 serving plates. Top with the cooked smoked salmon, cooked side up. Drizzle with the remaining dressing. Garnish with a few sprigs of fresh dill and a mixture of lemon, lime, and orange slices, then serve.

NUTRITION
Calories *115*; Sugars *1 g*; Protein *23 g*;
Carbohydrate *1 g*; Fat *15 g*; Saturates *2 g*

 ⭐⭐   easy
🕐   10 mins
🕐   6–9 mins

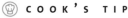 **COOK'S TIP**

This recipe would also work very well with smoked trout.

It is very important to use the freshest possible fish for this dish. The fish is not cooked, but cured with lemon and lime juice so that it has the appearance and texture of having been cooked.

Salmon Tartare

1 Cut the salmon into very tiny dice and season to taste with salt and pepper. Put into a large bowl.

2 Mix the lemon juice, lime juice, sugar, mustard, dill, basil, and olive oil together in another bowl. Pour over the salmon and mix well. Set aside for 15–20 minutes until the fish becomes opaque.

3 Meanwhile, mix the arugula, basil leaves, and salad greens together. Divide among 4 serving plates.

4 To serve, fill 4 small ramekins with the salmon mixture and turn out onto the center of the salad greens. Garnish with a few sprigs of fresh dill and basil leaves, then serve.

SERVES 4

2 lb/900 g very fresh salmon fillet, skinned
3 tbsp lemon juice
3 tbsp lime juice
2 tsp sugar
1 tsp Dijon mustard
1 tbsp chopped fresh dill
1 tbsp chopped fresh basil
2 tbsp olive oil
1¾ oz/50 g arugula
handful of fresh basil leaves
1¾ oz/50 g mixed salad greens
salt and pepper

to garnish
fresh dill sprigs
fresh basil leaves

NUTRITION
Calories *315*; Sugars *2 g*; Protein *31 g*;
Carbohydrate *2 g*; Fat *20 g*; Saturates *3 g*

    easy

   30 mins

   0 mins

🍴 **COOK'S TIP**

Haddock also responds very well to this treatment. Use half the quantity of salmon and an equal weight of haddock.

You need two pieces of salmon fillet for this dish, approximately the same size. Ask your fish market to remove all the bones and scale the fish for you.

Gravadlax

SERVES 4

2 salmon fillets, with skin on, about
   1 lb/450 g each
6 tbsp coarsely chopped fresh dill
¼ cup sea salt
¼ cup sugar
1 tbsp white peppercorns, coarsely crushed
12 slices brown bread, buttered, to serve

to garnish
lemon slices
fresh dill sprigs

1 Wash the salmon fillets under cold running water and pat dry with paper towels. Put 1 fillet, skin side down, in a non-metallic dish.

2 Mix the dill, sea salt, sugar, and peppercorns together. Spread this mixture over the first fillet of fish and place the second fillet, skin-side up, on top. Put a plate, the same size as the fish, on top and put a weight on the plate.

3 Let chill in the refrigerator for 2 days, turning the fish about every 12 hours and basting with any juices, that have come out of the fish.

4 Remove the salmon from the brine and slice thinly, without slicing the skin, as you would smoked salmon. Cut the brown bread into triangles. Arrange the salmon slices and brown bread on 4 serving plates and garnish with lemon slices and a few sprigs of fresh dill to serve.

NUTRITION
Calories *608*; Sugars *11 g*; Protein *37 g*;
Carbohydrate *41 g*; Fat *34 g*; Saturates *14 g*

 easy

 48 hrs

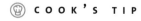 0 mins

🍴 **COOK'S TIP**

You can brush the marinade off the salmon before slicing, but the line of green along the edge of the salmon is quite attractive and, of course, full of flavor.

Don't be put off by the long list of ingredients. The omelet is served cold and so can be made entirely ahead of time.

Thai Crab Omelet

1 Put the crabmeat into a bowl and check for any small pieces of shell. Add the scallions, cilantro, chives, and cayenne and set aside.

2 Heat the vegetable oil in a large skillet over low heat. Add the garlic, ginger, and chile and stir-fry for 30 seconds. Add the lime juice, lime leaves, sugar, and Thai fish sauce. Let simmer for 3–4 minutes until reduced. Remove from the heat and let cool. Add to the crab mixture and set aside.

3 Lightly beat the eggs with the coconut cream and salt. Heat the vegetable oil in a large skillet over medium heat. Add the egg mixture and as it sets on the bottom, carefully pull the edges in toward the center, allowing the unset egg to run underneath.

4 When the egg is nearly set, spoon the crab mixture down the center. Cook for an additional 1–2 minutes to finish cooking the egg, then turn the omelet out of the skillet onto a serving dish. Let cool, then let chill in the refrigerator for 2–3 hours or overnight. Cut into 4 pieces and garnish with scallion slivers to serve.

SERVES 4

8 oz/225 g white crabmeat, fresh or thawed if frozen
3 scallions, chopped finely
1 tbsp chopped fresh cilantro
1 tbsp chopped fresh chives
pinch of cayenne pepper
1 tbsp vegetable oil
2 garlic cloves, crushed
1 tsp freshly grated gingerroot
1 fresh red chile, seeded and finely chopped
2 tbsp lime juice
2 lime leaves, shredded
2 tsp sugar
2 tsp Thai fish sauce
3 eggs
4 tbsp coconut cream
1 tsp salt
1 tbsp vegetable oil
scallion slivers, to garnish

NUTRITION
Calories *262*; Sugars *5 g*; Protein *18 g*; Carbohydrate *5 g*; Fat *19 g*; Saturates *7 g*

 moderate

 2 hrs 30 mins

35 mins

🍳 **COOK'S TIP**

You can serve this omelet warm. After adding the crab, cook for 3–4 minutes to let the mixture heat through, then serve immediately.

This is also known as Tom Yam Gung. Asian supermarkets may sell tom yam sauce ready prepared in jars, sometimes labeled "Chiles in Oil." This is a perfectly acceptable substitute and will certainly save on time.

Thai Fish Soup

SERVES 4

2 cups light chicken bouillon
2 kaffir lime leaves, chopped
2-inch/5-cm piece of lemongrass, chopped
3 tbsp lemon juice
3 tbsp Thai fish sauce
2 small, fresh hot green chiles, seeded and finely chopped
½ tsp sugar
8 small shiitake mushrooms or 8 straw mushrooms, halved
1 lb/450 g raw shrimp, peeled if necessary and deveined
shredded scallions, to garnish

tom yam sauce
4 tbsp vegetable oil
5 garlic cloves, finely chopped
1 large shallot, finely chopped
2 large hot dried red chilies, chopped coarsely
1 tbsp dried shrimp, optional
1 tbsp Thai fish sauce
2 tsp sugar

NUTRITION

Calories *230*; Sugars *4 g*; Protein *22 g*;
Carbohydrate *9 g*; Fat *12 g*; Saturates *1 g*

 moderate

25 mins

5 mins

1 To make the tom yam sauce, heat the vegetable oil in a small skillet over low heat. Add the garlic and cook for a few seconds until the garlic just browns. Remove with a draining spoon and set aside. Add the shallot to the same oil and cook until browned and crisp. Remove with a draining spoon and set aside. Add the chiles and cook until they darken. Remove from the oil and drain on paper towels. Remove from heat, reserving the oil.

2 Put the dried shrimp (if using) into a small food processor or spice grinder, and grind, then add the reserved chiles, garlic, and shallots. Grind to a smooth paste. Return the paste to the original skillet over low heat. Mix in the Thai fish sauce and sugar. Remove from the heat.

3 Heat the bouillon and 2 tablespoons of the tom yam sauce together in a large pan over low heat. Add the lime leaves, lemongrass, lemon juice, Thai fish sauce, chiles, and sugar. Let simmer for 2 minutes.

4 Add the mushrooms and shrimp and cook for another 2–3 minutes until the shrimp are cooked. Ladle into 4 warmed soup bowls, garnish with shredded scallions and serve immediately.

 COOK'S TIP

Some of the "kick" can be taken out of the chiles by removing the seeds and membrane. Cut fresh chiles in half and scrape out the seeds. Cut the ends off dried chilies and shake out the seeds. Wash your hands after handling chiles.

This delicious soup has a real "kick" of red-hot chiles, perfect to warm up a winter's day. If you prefer a milder flavor, remove the seeds from the chiles before using them.

Chile-Spiced Shrimp Wonton Soup

1 Finely chop the shrimp. Put them into a bowl and stir in the garlic, scallion, soy sauce, Thai fish sauce, cilantro, and egg yolk.

2 Lay the wonton wrappers on a counter in a single layer and place about 1 tablespoon of the filling mixture into the center of each. Brush the edges with egg white and fold each one into a triangle, pressing lightly to seal. Bring the 2 bottom corners of the triangle around to meet in the center, securing with a little egg white to hold in place.

3 To make the soup, slice the chiles on a steep diagonal angle to make long slices, removing the seeds, if you prefer. Slice the scallions on the same angle.

4 Place the bouillon, Thai fish sauce, soy sauce, and Chinese rice wine in a large pan and bring to a boil over medium heat. Add the chiles and scallions. Drop the wontons into the pan and let simmer for 4–5 minutes until thoroughly heated.

5 Ladle the soup and wontons into 4 small bowls, garnish with fresh cilantro leaves sprinkled over at the last moment and serve immediately.

SERVES 4

wontons
6 oz/175 g cooked peeled shrimp
1 garlic clove, crushed
1 scallion, chopped finely
1 tbsp dark soy sauce
1 tbsp Thai fish sauce
1 tbsp chopped fresh cilantro
1 small egg, separated
12 wonton wrappers

soup
2 small red bird's-eye chiles
2 scallions
4 cups clear beef bouillon
1 tbsp Thai fish sauce
1 tbsp dark soy sauce
1 tbsp Chinese rice wine
handful of fresh cilantro leaves, to garnish

NUTRITION
Calories *83*; Sugars *0.5 g*; Protein *13 g*;
Carbohydrate *4 g*; Fat *2 g*; Saturates *0.5 g*

 easy

 10 mins

8 mins

Hot-and-sour mixtures are popular throughout the East, especially in Thailand. This soup typically has either shrimp or chicken added, but tofu could be used instead if you prefer a vegetarian version.

Hot-*and*-Sour Soup

SERVES 4

12 oz/350 g whole raw or
  cooked shrimp in shell
1 tbsp vegetable oil
1 lemongrass stalk, chopped coarsely
2 kaffir lime leaves, shredded
1 fresh green chile, seeded and chopped
5 cups chicken or fish bouillon
1 lime
1 tbsp Thai fish sauce
salt and pepper
1 fresh red bird's-eye chile, seeded and sliced
1 scallion, sliced thinly
1 tbsp chopped fresh cilantro, to garnish

1 Peel the shrimp and set aside the shells. Devein the shrimp, cover and let chill in the refrigerator until required.

2 Heat the vegetable oil in a large skillet over medium heat. Add the shrimp shells and stir-fry for 3–4 minutes until they turn pink. Add the lemongrass, lime leaves, chile, and bouillon. Pare a strip of rind from the lime and grate the rest. Add the grated rind to the skillet.

3 Bring to a boil, then reduce the heat, cover and let simmer for 20 minutes.

4 Strain the liquid and pour it back into the skillet. Squeeze the juice from the lime and add to the skillet with the Thai fish sauce. Season to taste with salt and pepper.

5 Return to a boil, then reduce the heat, add the shrimp and let simmer for 2–3 minutes.

6 Add the thinly sliced chile and scallion. Ladle into 4 serving bowls, sprinkle with chopped cilantro and serve.

NUTRITION
Calories 71; Sugars 0 g; Protein 8 g;
Carbohydrate 1 g; Fat 4 g; Saturates 0 g

 easy

15 mins

30 mins

 COOK'S TIP

To devein the shrimp, remove the shells. Cut a slit along the back of each shrimp and remove the fine black vein that runs along the length of the back. Wipe with paper towels.

This is a traditional, creamy Scottish soup of smoked haddock and potato. As the smoked haddock has quite a strong flavor, it has been mixed with fresh cod.

Cullen Skink

1 Put the haddock fillet into a large skillet and cover with boiling water. Let stand for 10 minutes. Drain, reserving 1 cup of the soaking water. Flake the fish, taking care to remove all the bones.

2 Heat the butter in a large pan over low heat. Add the onion and cook gently for 10 minutes until softened. Add the milk and bring to a gentle simmer before adding the potato. Cook for 10 minutes.

3 Add the reserved haddock flakes and the cod. Let simmer for another 10 minutes until the cod is tender.

4 Remove about one third of the fish and potatoes, put into a food processor and process until smooth. Alternatively, rub through a strainer into a bowl. Return to the soup with the cream, parsley, and salt and pepper to taste. Taste and add a little lemon juice, if desired. Add a little of the reserved soaking water if the soup seems too thick. Reheat gently. Ladle into 4 warmed serving bowls, garnish with lemon slices and a few sprigs of fresh parsley, then serve immediately.

SERVES 4

8 oz/225 g smoked haddock fillet
2 tbsp butter
1 onion, chopped finely
2½ cups milk
12 oz/350 g potatoes, peeled and cut into dice
12 oz/350 g cod, boned, skinned, and cubed
⅔ cup heavy cream
2 tbsp chopped fresh parsley
lemon juice, to taste
salt and pepper

to garnish
lemon slices
fresh parsley sprigs

NUTRITION
Calories *108*; Sugars *2.3 g*; Protein *7.4 g*; Carbohydrate *5.6 g*; Fat *6.4 g*; Saturates *4 g*

moderate

20 mins

40 mins

COOK'S TIP

Choose Finnan haddock, if you can find it. Traditionally cured over peat smoke, it can also be eaten by itself or used in omelets or dishes such as kedgeree.

A chowder is a thick soup; the main ingredients are milk and potatoes, to which other flavors are added. This is a classic version from New England, flavored with fresh clams.

New England Clam Chowder

SERVES 4

2 lb/900 g live clams
4 bacon slices, chopped
2 tbsp butter
1 onion, chopped
1 tbsp chopped fresh thyme
1 large potato, peeled and diced
1 bay leaf
1¼ cups milk
1⅔ cup heavy cream
1 tbsp chopped fresh parsley
salt and pepper

1 Scrub the clams and put into a large pan with a splash of water. Cook over high heat for 3–4 minutes until all the clams have opened. Discard any that remain closed. Strain the clams, reserving the cooking liquid. Set aside until cool enough to handle.

2 Set aside 8 clams in the shells for garnish, then remove the rest of the clams from their shells. Coarsely chop if large and set aside.

3 Dry-fry the bacon in a clean pan over medium–low heat until browned and crisp. Drain on paper towels. Add the butter to the same pan and when it has melted, add the onion. Cook for 4–5 minutes until softened, but not colored. Add the thyme and cook briefly before adding the diced potato, reserved clam cooking liquid, milk, and bay leaf. Bring to a boil and let simmer for 10 minutes until the potato is tender, but not falling apart. Transfer to a food processor and process until smooth. Alternatively, rub through a strainer into a bowl and return to the pan.

4 Add the clams, bacon, and cream. Let simmer for another 2–3 minutes until heated through. Season to taste with salt and pepper. Stir in the parsley and ladle into 4 soup bowls. Garnish with the reserved clams and serve.

NUTRITION
Calories 136; Sugars 2 g; Protein 7.7 g;
Carbohydrate 5.4 g; Fat 9.5 g; Saturates 5.4 g

 easy

15 mins

 30 mins

COOK'S TIP

For a smart presentation, set aside 8 clams in their shells. Sit 2 on top of each bowl of soup to serve.

Packed full of flavor, this delicious fish soup makes a meal in itself when it is ideal accompanied by mixed salad greens.

Fish *and* Crab Chowder

1 Place the onion, celery, and wine in a large non-stick pan. Bring to a boil, cover and cook over low heat for 5 minutes.

2 Uncover the pan and cook for another 5 minutes until almost all the liquid has evaporated.

3 Pour in the bouillon and milk, and add the bay leaf. Bring to a simmer and stir in the cod and haddock. Let simmer over low heat, uncovered, for 5 minutes.

4 Add the crabmeat, beans, and cooked brown rice and let simmer gently for 2–3 minutes until just heated through. Remove the bay leaf with a draining spoon and discard.

5 Stir in the cornstarch mixture and heat, stirring, until thickened slightly. Season to taste with salt and pepper and ladle into 4 large, warmed soup bowls. Serve with mixed salad greens.

SERVES 4

1 large onion, chopped finely
2 celery stalks, chopped finely
⅔ cup dry white wine
2½ cups fish bouillon
2½ cups skim milk
1 bay leaf
8 oz/225 g smoked cod fillet, skinned and cut into 1-inch/2.5-cm cubes
8 oz/225 g smoked haddock fillets, skinned and cut into 1-inch/2.5-cm cubes
12 oz/350 g canned crabmeat, drained
8 oz/225 g blanched green beans, sliced into 1-inch/2.5-cm pieces
2 cups cooked brown rice
4 tsp cornstarch mixed with 4 tbsp water
salt and pepper
mixed salad greens, to serve

NUTRITION
Calories *440*; Sugars *10 g*; Protein *49 g*; Carbohydrate *43 g*; Fat *7 g*; Saturates *1 g*

easy
40 mins
25 mins

This soup is based on the classic Chinese chicken and corn soup, but the delicate flavor of the crab works very well.

Chinese Crab *and* Corn Soup

SERVES 4

1 tbsp vegetable oil
1 small onion, chopped finely
1 garlic clove, chopped finely
1 tsp grated fresh gingerroot
1 small, fresh red chile, seeded
   and finely chopped
2 tbsp dry sherry or Chinese rice wine
8 oz/225 g fresh white crabmeat
11 oz/320 g canned corn, drained
2½ cups light chicken bouillon
1 tbsp light soy sauce
2 tbsp chopped fresh cilantro
2 eggs, beaten
salt and pepper
fresh red chile tassels, to garnish

1 Heat the vegetable oil in a large pan over low heat. Add the onion and cook gently for 5 minutes until softened. Add the garlic, ginger, and chile and cook for another 1 minute.

2 Add the sherry or Chinese rice wine and bubble until reduced by half. Add the crabmeat, corn, chicken bouillon, and soy sauce. Bring to a boil and let simmer gently for 5 minutes. Stir in the cilantro. Season to taste with salt and pepper.

3 Remove from the heat and pour in the eggs. Wait for a few seconds and then stir well, to break the eggs into ribbons. Ladle into 4 large, warmed soup bowls, garnish with fresh chile tassels and serve immediately.

NUTRITION
Calories *440 g*; Sugars *10 g*; Protein *49 g*;
Carbohydrate *43 g*; Fat *7 g*; Saturates *1 g*

easy

40 mins

25 mins

 **COOK'S TIP**

For convenience, you could use canned crabmeat. Make sure it is well drained before adding it to the soup.

This is a very delicately flavored soup which, like all seafood, should not be overcooked. A sprinkling of fresh parsley just before serving makes a pretty contrast to the creamy color of the soup.

Creamy Scallop Soup

1 Melt the butter in a large pan over low heat. Add the onion and cook very gently for 10 minutes until the onions are softened, but not colored. Add the potatoes and salt and pepper to taste, cover and cook for another 10 minutes.

2 Pour on the hot fish bouillon, bring to a boil and let simmer for another 10–15 minutes until the potatoes are tender.

3 Meanwhile, prepare the scallops. If the corals are available, coarsely chop and set aside. Coarsely chop the white meat and put into a second pan with the milk. Bring to a simmer and cook for 6–8 minutes until the scallops are just tender.

4 When the potatoes are cooked, transfer them and their cooking liquid to a food processor or blender and process to a purée. Alternatively, rub through a strainer. Return the mixture to a clean pan with the scallops and their milk and the pieces of coral (if using).

5 Remove the pan from the heat. Whisk the egg yolks and cream together and add to the soup. Return to a very low heat and, stirring constantly, reheat the soup until thickened slightly. Do not boil or it will curdle. Adjust the seasoning to taste. Ladle into 4 soup bowls, sprinkle with parsley and serve.

 COOK'S TIP

The soup can be made in advance up to the point where the cream and eggs are added. This should only be done just before serving.

SERVES 4

¼ cup butter
1 onion, chopped finely
1 lb/450 g potatoes, peeled and diced
2½ cups hot fish bouillon
12 oz/350 g prepared scallops, including corals if available
1¼ cups milk
2 egg yolks
¾ cup heavy cream
salt and pepper
1 tbsp chopped fresh parsley, to garnish

NUTRITION
Calories 9.8; Sugars 1.4 g; Protein 6.5 g; Carbohydrate 5.9 g; Fat 5.6 g; Saturates 3.2 g

easy
40 mins
35 mins

Surprisingly, this soup is French in origin. This version, however, uses freshly roasted spices rather than the bland curry powder that is so popular.

Curried Mussel Soup

SERVES 4

½ tsp coriander seeds
½ tsp cumin seeds
2 lb/900 g live mussels
scant ½ cup white wine
¼ cup butter
1 onion, chopped finely
1 garlic clove, chopped finely
1 tsp freshly grated gingerroot
1 tsp turmeric
pinch of cayenne pepper
2½ cups fish bouillon
4 tbsp heavy cream
2 tbsp butter, softened
2 tbsp all-purpose flour
salt and pepper
2 tbsp chopped fresh cilantro, to garnish

NUTRITION

Calories *391*; Sugars *3 g*; Protein *11 g*;
Carbohydrate *11 g*; Fat *32 g*; Saturates *20 g*

easy

45 mins

30 mins

1 Dry-fry the coriander and cumin seeds in a skillet over medium heat until they start to smell aromatic and begin to pop. Transfer to a mortar and grind to a powder with a pestle. Set aside.

2 Clean the mussels by scrubbing or scraping the shells and pulling out any beards that are attached to them. Discard any with broken shells or any that refuse to close when tapped. Put the mussels into a large pan with the wine and cook, covered, over high heat for 3–4 minutes, shaking the pan occasionally, until all the mussels have opened. Discard any mussels that remain closed. Strain, reserving the cooking liquid, and set aside until the mussels are cool enough to handle. Remove about two thirds of the mussels from their shells and set them all aside. Strain the mussel cooking liquid through a fine strainer.

3 Heat half the butter in a pan over low heat. Add the onion and cook gently for 4–5 minutes until softened, but not colored. Add the garlic and ginger and cook for another 1 minute before adding the roasted and ground spices, the turmeric, and cayenne. Cook for 1 minute before adding the fish bouillon, reserved mussel cooking liquid, and cream. Let simmer for 10 minutes.

4 Cream the butter and flour together to form a thick paste. Add the paste to the simmering soup and stir until dissolved and until the soup has thickened slightly. Add the mussels and warm for 2 minutes. Ladle into 4 warmed soup bowls, garnish with parsley and serve.

This recipe is intended to be served in small quantities. It is very rich and full of flavor.

Clam *and* Sorrel Soup

1 Put the clams into a large pan with the onion and wine. Cover and cook over high heat for 3–4 minutes until the clams have opened. Strain, reserving the cooking liquid, but discarding the onion. Set aside the clams until they are cool enough to handle. Remove from their shells.

2 Melt the butter in a clean pan over low heat. Add the carrot, shallots, and celery and cook very gently for 10 minutes until softened, but not colored. Add the reserved cooking liquid and bay leaves and let simmer for another 10 minutes.

3 Meanwhile, coarsely chop the clams, if large. Add to the soup with the cream and sorrel. Let simmer for another 2–3 minutes until the sorrel has collapsed. Season with pepper and ladle into 4 warmed soup bowls. Garnish with a few sprigs of fresh dill and serve immediately.

S E R V E S 4

2 lb/900 g live clams, scrubbed
1 onion, chopped finely
²⁄₃ cup dry white wine
¼ cup butter
1 small carrot, diced finely
2 shallots, diced finely
1 celery stalk, diced finely
2 bay leaves
²⁄₃ cup heavy cream
1 cup loosely packed shredded sorrel
pepper
fresh dill sprigs, to garnish

N U T R I T I O N
Calories *384*; Sugars *4 g*; Protein *18 g*;
Carbohydrate *7 g*; Fat *29 g*; Saturates *18 g*

✪✪✪   moderate
🍥   10–15 mins
🕐   30 mins

 COOK'S TIP

Sorrel is a large-leaf herb with a slightly sour, lemony flavor that goes very well with fish. It is increasingly easy to find in larger supermarkets, but is also incredibly easy to grow as a plant.

Use any type of fish that is available for this soup. Good fish to choose might include eel, skate, or cod. Avoid oily fish such as mackerel, herring, and salmon.

Fish *and* Bread Soup

SERVES 6 – 8

4 lb/1.7 kg mixed whole fish
8 oz/225 g raw shrimp, shell on
10 cups water
⅔ cup olive oil
2 large onions, chopped coarsely
2 celery sticks, chopped coarsely
1 leek, chopped coarsely
1 small fennel bulb, chopped coarsely
5 garlic cloves, chopped
3 tbsp. orange juice, plus 1 strip orange peel
14 oz/400 g canned chopped tomatoes
1 red bell pepper, seeded and sliced
1 fresh thyme sprig
large pinch of saffron theads
6–8 thick slices sourdough bread
salt and pepper

saffron sauce
1 red bell pepper, seeded and cut into fourths
⅔ cup olive oil
1 egg yolk
large pinch of saffron threads
pinch of chili flakes

NUTRITION

Calories *755*; Sugars *9 g*; Protein *46 g*;
Carbohydrate *23 g*; Fat *54 g*; Saturates *9 g*

⭐⭐   easy

🕐   40 mins

🕐   1 hr 10 mins

1 Fillet the fish and set aside all the bones. Coarsely chop the flesh. Peel the shrimp. Place the fish bones and the shells in a large pan with the water and bring to a boil over medium heat. Let simmer for 20 minutes, then strain.

2 Heat the olive oil in a large pan over low heat. Add the onions, celery, leek, fennel, and garlic and cook gently for 20 minutes without coloring. Add the orange peel and juice, tomatoes, red bell pepper, thyme, saffron, shrimp, and fish fillets and bouillon, bring to a boil and let simmer for 40 minutes.

3 To prepare the sauce. Brush the red bell pepper fourths with some of the olive oil. Cook under a hot preheated broiler for 8–10 minutes, turning once, until the skins are charred and blistered and the flesh is tender. Put into a plastic bag.

4 Once cool, peel off the skin. Coarsely chop the flesh and place in a food processor with the egg yolk, saffron, chili flakes, and seasoning. Process until the bell pepper is smooth. Add the olive oil, in a slow stream, until the sauce starts to thicken. Continue adding the oil in a steady stream until all the oil is incorporated. Season to taste with salt and pepper, if necessary.

5 When the soup is cooked, put into a food processor or blender and process until smooth, then rub through a strainer. Return to the heat and season to taste with salt and pepper.

6 Toast the bread on both sides and place in the bottom of the soup plates. Ladle over the soup and serve with the sauce.

Although versions of this stew are eaten throughout Spain, it originated in the Basque region and would have been largely prepared and eaten by fishermen.

Basque Tuna Stew

1 Heat 2 tablespoons of the oil in a pan over low heat. Add the onion and cook for 8–10 minutes until softened and browned. Add the garlic and cook for another 1 minute. Add the tomatoes, cover and let simmer for 30 minutes until thickened.

2 Meanwhile, mix the potatoes and peppers together in a clean pan. Add the water, which should just cover the vegetables. Bring to a boil and let simmer for 15 minutes until the potatoes are almost tender.

3 Add the tuna chunks and the tomato mixture to the potatoes and peppers and season to taste with salt and pepper. Cover and let simmer for 6–8 minutes until the tuna is tender.

4 Meanwhile, heat the remaining olive oil in a large skillet over medium heat. Add the bread slices and cook on both sides until golden. Drain on paper towels. Transfer the stew to 4 large, warmed serving bowls and serve with the toast, if desired.

SERVES 4

5 tbsp olive oil
1 large onion, chopped
2 garlic cloves, chopped
7 oz/200 g canned chopped tomatoes
1 lb 9 oz/700 g potatoes, peeled and cut into 2-inch/5-cm chunks
3 green bell peppers, seeded and coarsely chopped
1¼ cups cold water
2 lb/900 g fresh tuna, cut into chunks
4 slices crusty white bread, optional
salt and pepper

NUTRITION
Calories *718*; Sugars *9 g*; Protein *63 g*; Carbohydrate *2 g*; Fat *6 g*; Saturates *1 g*

 easy
5 mins
20 mins

COOK'S TIP

Substitute any very firm-fleshed fish, such as shark or swordfish, for the tuna used in this recipe.

Goan cuisine is famous for seafood and vindaloo dishes, which tend to be very hot. This is a milder dish, but also very flavorful.

Goan Fish Curry

SERVES 4

1 lb/10 oz/750 g monkfish fillet, cut into chunks
1 tbsp cider vinegar
½ tsp salt
1 tsp ground turmeric
3 tbsp vegetable oil
2 garlic cloves, crushed
1 small onion, chopped finely
2 tsp ground coriander
1 tsp cayenne pepper
2 tsp paprika
2 tbsp tamarind pulp plus 2 tbsp boiling water (see method)
3 oz/85 g creamed coconut, cut into pieces
1¼ cups warm water
1 tbsp chopped fresh cilantro, to garnish
plain boiled rice, to serve

NUTRITION
Calories 302; Sugars 7 g; Protein 31 g;
Carbohydrate 8 g; Fat 17 g; Saturates 7 g

   easy
   30 mins
   12 mins

1 Put the fish on a plate and drizzle over the vinegar. Mix the salt and half the turmeric together and sprinkle evenly over the fish. Cover and set aside for 20 minutes.

2 Heat the vegetable oil in a skillet over low heat. Add the garlic and cook until browned slightly, then add the onion and cook for 3–4 minutes until softened, but not browned. Add the ground coriander and stir for 1 minute.

3 Mix the remaining turmeric, cayenne, and paprika with about 2 tablespoons of water to make a paste. Add to the skillet and cook over low heat for about 1–2 minutes.

4 Mix the tamarind pulp with the boiling water and stir well. When the water appears thick and the pulp has come away from the seeds, rub this mixture through a strainer, rubbing the pulp well. Discard the seeds once finished.

5 Add the coconut, warm water, and tamarind paste to the skillet and stir until the coconut has dissolved. Add the pieces of fish and any juices on the plate and let simmer gently for 4–5 minutes until the sauce has thickened and the fish is just tender. Garnish with cilantro and serve immediately, on a bed of plain boiled rice.

The pale green curry paste in this recipe can be used as the basis for all sorts of Thai fish dishes. It is also delicious with chicken and beef.

Thai Green Fish Curry

1 To make the curry paste. Put all the ingredients into a blender or spice grinder and blend to a smooth paste, adding a little water, if necessary. Alternatively, pound the ingredients, using a mortar and pestle, until smooth. Set aside.

2 Heat the vegetable oil in a large skillet or preheated wok over medium heat until almost smoking. Add the garlic and stir-fry until golden. Add the curry paste and stir-fry a few seconds before adding the eggplant. Stir-fry for about 4–5 minutes until softened.

3 Add the coconut cream, bring to a boil and stir until the cream thickens and curdles slightly. Add the Thai fish sauce and sugar to the skillet and stir well.

4 Add the fish pieces and bouillon. Let simmer for 3–4 minutes, stirring occasionally, until the fish is just tender. Add the lime leaves and basil, and then cook for another 1 minute. Transfer to a large, warmed serving dish and garnish with a few sprigs of fresh dill. Serve immediately.

SERVES 4

2 tbsp vegetable oil
1 garlic clove, chopped
1 small eggplant, diced
½ cup coconut cream
2 tbsp Thai fish sauce
1 tsp sugar
8 oz/225 g firm white fish, cut into pieces
½ cup fish bouillon
2 kaffir lime leaves, shredded finely
about 15 leaves fresh Thai basil, if available
fresh dill sprigs, to garnish

green curry paste
5 fresh green chiles, seeded and chopped
2 tsp chopped lemongrass
1 large shallot, chopped
2 garlic cloves, chopped
1 tsp freshly grated gingerroot or galangal
2 fresh coriander roots, chopped
½ tsp ground coriander
¼ tsp ground cumin
1 kaffir lime leaf, chopped finely
½ tsp salt

NUTRITION
Calories *217*; Sugars *3 g*; Protein *12 g*; Carbohydrate *5 g*; Fat *17 g*; Saturates *10 g*

  easy

45 mins

15 mins

Although the word escabeche is Spanish in origin, variations of this dish are cooked all over the Mediterranean.

Mackerel Escabeche

SERVES 4

⅔ cup olive oil
4 mackerel, filleted
2 tbsp all-purpose flour, for dusting
4 tbsp red wine vinegar
1 onion, sliced finely
1 strip of orange rind, removed with
   a potato peeler
1 fresh thyme sprig
1 fresh rosemary sprig
1 bay leaf
4 garlic cloves, minced
2 fresh red chiles, bruised
1 tsp salt
3 tbsp chopped fresh Italian parsley
salt and pepper
1 fresh red chile, sliced lengthwise,
   to garnish

1 Heat half the olive oil in a skillet over medium heat. Put the flour onto a plate and season with salt and pepper. Dust the mackerel fillets with the seasoned flour.

2 Add the fish to the skillet and cook for about 30 seconds on each side until not quite cooked through.

3 Transfer the mackerel to a shallow dish, large enough to hold the fillets in a single layer.

4 Add the the vinegar, onion, orange rind, thyme, rosemary, bay leaf, garlic, chiles, and salt to the skillet. Let simmer for 10 minutes.

5 Add the remaining olive oil and the chopped parsley. Pour the mixture over the fish and leave until cold. Transfer to a large serving plate, garnish with a chile and serve.

NUTRITION
Calories 750; Sugars 3 g; Protein 33 g;
Carbohydrate 12 g; Fat 63 g; Saturates 11 g

  easy
  3 hrs
  12–14 mins

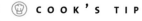 **COOK'S TIP**

Substitute 12 whole sardines, cleaned, with heads removed, for the mackerel. Cook in the same way. Tuna steaks are also delicious served escabeche.

This is a popular way to serve fish in the Middle East. The fish is first deep-fried and then served with a delicious sauce of onions, tomatoes, nuts, and lots of fresh parsley.

Lemon Sole *in a* Sweet *and* Sour Sauce

1 Wash the fish fillets under cold running water and pat dry with paper towels. Dredge lightly with flour. Heat about 1 inch/2.5 cm of olive oil—enough to just cover the fish—in a large skillet over medium–high heat. Add the fish fillets, 2 at a time, and completely submerge in the oil. Cook for 5–6 minutes, then drain on paper towels. Set aside. Cook the remaining fish the same way.

2 Heat the remaining 2 tablespoons of olive oil in a large pan over low heat. Add the onions and cook for 7–8 minutes until softened and starting to brown. Add the hazelnuts, pine nuts, and raisins and cook for another 1–2 minutes until the nuts are golden. Add the tomatoes and cook for 5 minutes until softened.

3 Add the vinegar and let simmer for 5 minutes. Add the water, parsley, and salt and pepper to taste and stir well. Let simmer for another 5 minutes.

4 Lower the fried fish into the sauce and let simmer gently for 10 minutes. Transfer to 4 large, warmed serving plates and garnish with a few sprigs of fresh dill and lemon slices. Serve with boiled new potatoes and green beans.

SERVES 4

2 large lemon sole, filleted
1–2 tbsp all-purpose flour, to dredge
2 cups olive oil, for deep-frying,
    plus 2 tbsp olive oil
2 onions, sliced thinly
1 cup hazelnuts, chopped
½ cup pine nuts
¼ cup raisins
8 oz/225 g ripe tomatoes, peeled,
    and chopped
2 tbsp red wine vinegar
½ cup water
3 tbsp chopped fresh parsley
salt and pepper

to garnish
fresh dill sprigs
lemon slices

to serve
boiled new potatoes
freshly cooked green beans

NUTRITION
Calories *528*; Sugars *16 g*; Protein *23 g*;
Carbohydrate *21 g*; Fat *40 g*; Saturates *4 g*

★★   easy
      20 mins
     50 mins

🍳 **COOK'S TIP**

In the Middle East, many different types of fish are treated this way, but a particular favorite is red mullet. Small fish can be left whole (after cleaning and scaling).

This is a very simple dish which uses a variety of spices and ingredients readily available.

Haddock Baked *in* Yogurt

SERVES 4

2 large onions, sliced thinly
2 lb/900 g haddock fillet, from the head end
scant 2 cups plain yogurt
2 tbsp lemon juice
1 tsp sugar
2 tsp ground cumin
2 tsp ground coriander
pinch of garam masala
pinch of cayenne pepper, to taste
1 tsp freshly grated gingerroot
3 tbsp vegetable oil
¼ cup cold unsalted butter, cut into pieces
salt and pepper
fresh parsley sprigs, to garnish

to serve
boiled new potatoes
freshly cooked snow peas

1 Line a large baking dish with the onion slices. Cut the fish into strips widthwise and lay the fish in a single layer over the onions.

2 Mix the yogurt, lemon juice, sugar, cumin, coriander, garam masala, cayenne, ginger, vegetable oil and seasoning together in a bowl. Pour the sauce over the fish, making sure it goes under the fish as well. Cover tightly.

3 Bake in a preheated oven, 375°F/190°C, for 30 minutes or until the fish is just tender. Remove from the oven.

4 Carefully pour the sauce off the fish and into a pan. Bring to a boil over low heat and let simmer to reduce the sauce to 1½ cups. Remove from the heat.

5 Add the cubes of butter to the sauce and whisk until melted and incorporated. Pour the sauce back over the fish and transfer to 4 large, warmed serving plates and serve with boiled new potatoes and snow peas.

NUTRITION
Calories *448*; Sugars *16 g*; Protein *47 g*; Carbohydrate *20 g*; Fat *21 g*; Saturates *8 g*

  easy
20 mins
  40 mins

COOK'S TIP

When you pour the sauce off the fish it will look thin and separated, but reducing and stirring in the butter will help to thicken it.

Not strictly authentic, but this dish uses the typical Italian flavors of tomatoes, capers, olives, and basil to make a simple but delicious supper dish.

Cod Italienne

1 Heat the olive oil in a large pan over low heat. Add the onion and cook gently for 5 minutes until softened, but not colored. Add the garlic and thyme and cook for another 1 minute.

2 Add the wine and increase the heat. Let simmer until reduced and syrupy. Add the tomatoes and sugar and bring to a boil. Cover and let simmer for 30 minutes. Uncover and let simmer for another 20 minutes until thick. Stir in the olives, capers, and basil. Season to taste with salt and pepper.

3 Arrange the cod steaks in a shallow ovenproof dish and spoon the tomato sauce over the top. Bake in a preheated oven, 375°F/190°C, for 20–25 minutes until the fish is just tender.

4 Remove from the oven and arrange the mozzarella slices on top of the fish.

5 Return to the oven for another 5–10 minutes until the cheese has melted. Transfer to 4 large, warmed serving plates and garnish with a few sprigs of cilantro and lime slices. Serve immediately.

SERVES 4

2 tbsp olive oil
1 onion, chopped finely
2 garlic clove, chopped finely
2 tsp freshly chopped thyme
²⁄₃ cup red wine
14 oz/400 g canned chopped tomatoes
pinch of sugar
¼ cup pitted black olives, coarsely chopped
¼ cup pitted green olives, coarsely chopped
2 tbsp capers, drained, rinsed, and coarsely chopped
2 tbsp chopped fresh basil
4 cod steaks, about 6 oz/175 g each
5½ oz/150 g buffalo mozzarella cheese, sliced
salt and pepper

to garnish
fresh cilantro sprigs
lime slices

NUTRITION
Calories *387*; Sugars *8 g*; Protein *44 g*;
Carbohydrate *10 g*; Fat *16 g*; Saturates *6 g*

 easy

 15 mins

1 hr 30 mins

🐱 **COOK'S TIP**

Other white fish steaks would work equally well—for a luxury alternative, try halibut.

Although not strictly authentic, the use of curry paste in this recipe makes it very quick and easy to prepare.

Cod Curry

SERVES 4

1 tbsp vegetable oil

1 small onion, chopped

2 garlic cloves, chopped

1-inch/2.5-cm piece of fresh gingerroot, chopped coarsely

2 large ripe tomatoes, peeled and coarsely chopped

²/₃ cup fish bouillon

1 tbsp medium curry paste

1 tsp ground coriander

14 oz/400 g canned garbanzo beans, drained and rinsed

1 lb 10 oz/750 g cod fillet, cut into large chunks

4 tbsp chopped fresh cilantro

4 tbsp plain yogurt

salt and pepper

steamed basmati rice, to serve

1 Heat the vegetable oil in a large pan over low heat. Add the onion, garlic, and ginger and cook for 4–5 minutes until softened. Remove from the heat. Put the onion mixture into a food processor or blender with the tomatoes and fish bouillon and process until smooth.

2 Return to the pan with the curry paste, ground coriander, and garbanzo beans. Mix well, then let simmer gently for 15 minutes until thickened.

3 Add the pieces of fish and return to a simmer. Cook for 5 minutes until the fish is just tender. Remove from the heat and let stand for 2–3 minutes.

4 Stir in the cilantro and yogurt. Season to taste with salt and pepper and serve with steamed basmati rice.

NUTRITION
Calories 310; Sugars 4 g; Protein 42 g; Carbohydrate 19 g; Fat 8 g; Saturates 1 g

easy

40 mins

25 mins

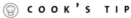

COOK'S TIP

Instead of using the cod, make this curry using raw shrimp and omit the garbanzo beans.

You will need to start preparing this dish two days ahead to allow for salting the cod.

Home-Salted Cod *with* Garbanzo Beans

1 Sprinkle the salt over both sides of the cod fillet. Place in a shallow dish, cover and let chill in the refrigerator for 48 hours. When ready to cook, remove the cod from the refrigerator and rinse under cold running water. Let soak in cold water for 2 hours.

2 Drain the garbanzo beans, rinse them thoroughly, and drain again. Put into a large pan, add double their volume of water and bring slowly to a boil. Skim away any froth that rises to the surface with a draining spoon. Split the chile lengthwise and add to the garbanzo beans with the whole garlic cloves and bay leaves. Bring to a boil and boil fast for 15 minutes. Cover and let simmer for 1½–2 hours until very tender, skimming occasionally, if necessary.

3 Drain the cod and pat dry with paper towels. Brush with the olive oil and season well with pepper, but no salt. Cook under a preheated hot broiler or on a preheated hot, ridged griddle for 3–4 minutes on each side until tender. Meanwhile, add the chicken bouillon to the garbanzo beans and bring back to a boil. Keep warm.

4 To make the gremolata, mix the parsley, garlic, and finely grated lemon rind together in a small bowl.

5 To serve, ladle the garbanzo beans and their cooking liquid into 6 warmed soup bowls. Top with the broiled cod and sprinkle over the gremolata. Drizzle generously with olive oil, garnish with bay leaves and serve immediately.

SERVES 6

¼ cup sea salt
3 lb 5oz/1.5 kg fresh boneless cod fillet, from the head end, skin on
8 oz/225 g dried garbanzo beans, soaked overnight
1 fresh red chile
4 garlic cloves
2 bay leaves, plus extra to garnish
1 tbsp olive oil
1¼ cups chicken bouillon
pepper
1 tbsp extra virgin olive oil, to drizzle
a few bay leaves, to garnish

gremolata
3 tbsp chopped fresh parsley
2 garlic cloves, chopped finely
finely grated rind of 1 lemon

NUTRITION
Calories *283*; Sugars *0 g*; Protein *39 g*; Carbohydrate *7 g*; Fat *7 g*; Saturates *1 g*

  moderate
  50 hrs
  2 hrs 30 mins

This is a rich and flavorful stew of slowly cooked squid in a sauce of tomatoes and red wine, cooked slowly so that the squid becomes very tender.

Squid Stew

SERVES 4

1 lb 10 oz/750 g squid
3 tbsp olive oil
1 onion, chopped
3 garlic cloves, chopped finely
1 tsp fresh thyme leaves
14 oz/400 g canned chopped tomatoes
²⁄₃ cup red wine
1¼ cups water
1 tbsp chopped fresh parsley
salt and pepper

to garnish
fresh dill sprigs
lemon slices

1 To prepare whole squid, hold the body firmly and grasp the tentacles just inside the body. Pull firmly to remove the innards. Find the transparent "backbone" and remove. Grasp the wings on the outside of the body and pull to remove the outer skin. Trim the tentacles just below the beak and reserve. Wash the body and tentacles under cold running water. Slice the body into rings. Drain well on paper towels.

2 Heat the olive oil in a large, ovenproof casserole over medium heat. Add the prepared squid and cook, stirring occasionally, until lightly browned.

3 Reduce the heat and add the onion, garlic, and thyme. Cook for another 5 minutes until softened.

4 Stir in the tomatoes, red wine, and water. Bring to a boil and let simmer gently for 2 hours. Stir in the parsley and season to taste with salt and pepper. Transfer to a large, warmed serving dish and garnish with a few sprigs of fresh dill and lemon slices. Serve immediately.

NUTRITION
Calories *284*; Sugars *5 g*; Protein *31 g*;
Carbohydrate *9 g*; Fat *12 g*; Saturates *2 g*

★★★   moderate
     20 mins
     2 hours 15 mins

🎩 **COOK'S TIP**

This dish can be used as the basis of a more substantial stew. Before adding the parsley, add extra seafood such as scallops, pieces of fish fillet, or jumbo shrimp. Return to a boil and cook for 2 minutes. Add the parsley and seasoning.

This is an impressive-looking Catalan dish with two classics of Spanish cooking— the *sofrito*, a slow-cooked mixture of vegetables, and the *picada*, usually nuts, bread, and garlic, used to finish and thicken the stew.

Spanish Fish Stew

1 Heat 3 tablespoons of the olive oil in a skillet over low heat. Add the onions and cook gently for 10–15 minutes until lightly golden, adding a little water to prevent them sticking, if necessary. Add the tomatoes and cook until they have melted down and the oil has separated away from them.

2 Heat 1 tablespoon of the remaining olive oil in a separate skillet over medium heat. Add bread slices and cook until crisp. Break into coarse pieces and put into a mortar with the almonds and 2 garlic cloves. Pound together to make a fine paste. Alternatively, process in a food processor.

3 Split the lobster lengthwise. Remove and discard the intestinal vein, which runs down the tail, the stomach sac, and the gills. Crack the claws and remove the meat. Remove the flesh from the tail and chop into large chunks.

4 Season the monkfish, cod, and lobster with salt and pepper and dust with a little flour. Heat a little of the remaining olive oil in a skillet. Add the fish separately: monkfish, cod, lobster, then squid, shrimp, and langoustines and brown, then arrange in an ovenproof casserole.

5 Add the mussels, clams, remaining garlic, and parsley to the casserole and place over low heat. Pour over the brandy and ignite. When the flames have died down, add the tomato mixture and just enough water to cover. Bring to a boil and let simmer for 3–4 minutes until the mussels and clams have opened. Discard any that remain closed. Stir in the bread and season to taste with salt and pepper. Let simmer for another 5 minutes until all the fish is tender. Transfer to 6 serving plates and garnish with lemon to serve.

SERVES 6

5 tbsp olive oil
2 large onions, chopped finely
2 ripe tomatoes, peeled, seeded, and diced
2 slices white bread, crusts removed
4 almonds, toasted
3 garlic cloves, chopped coarsely
12 oz/350 g cooked lobster
7 oz/200 g monkfish fillet
7 oz/200 g cod fillet, skinned
7 oz/200 g cleaned squid, cut into rings
1 tbsp all-purpose flour
6 large jumbo shrimp
6 langoustines
18 live mussels, scrubbed, beards removed
8 large live clams, scrubbed
1 tbsp chopped fresh parsley
½ cup brandy
salt and pepper
lemon slices, to garnish

NUTRITION
Calories 346; Sugars 4 g; Protein 37 g; Carbohydrate 11 g; Fat 13 g; Saturates 2 g

 challenging
30 mins
40 mins

A tagine is a Moroccan cooking vessel consisting of an earthenware dish with a domed lid that has a steam hole in the top. However, this dish can be made quite successfully in an ordinary pan.

Moroccan Fish Tagine

SERVES 4

2 tbsp olive oil
1 large onion, chopped finely
large pinch of saffron strands
½ tsp ground cinnamon
1 tsp ground coriander
½ tsp ground cumin
½ tsp ground turmeric
7 oz/200 g canned chopped tomatoes
1¼ cups fish bouillon
4 small red mullet cleaned, boned, and
   heads and tails removed
½ cup pitted green olives
1 tbsp chopped preserved lemon
   (see Cook's Tip)
3 tbsp chopped fresh cilantro
salt and pepper

1 Heat the olive oil in a large pan or ovenproof casserole over low heat. Add the onion and cook gently for 10 minutes until softened, but not colored. Add the saffron, cinnamon, coriander, cumin, and turmeric and cook for another 30 seconds, stirring.

2 Add the chopped tomatoes and fish bouillon and stir well. Bring to a boil, cover and let simmer for 15 minutes. Uncover and let simmer for another 20–35 minutes until thickened.

3 Cut each red mullet in half, then add the pieces to the pan, pushing them into the sauce. Let simmer gently for another 5–6 minutes until the fish is just cooked.

4 Carefully stir in the olives, preserved lemon, and the chopped cilantro. Season to taste with salt and pepper and serve immediately.

NUTRITION
Calories *188*; Sugars *5 g*; Protein *17 g*;
Carbohydrate *7 g*; Fat *11 g*; Saturates *1 g*

⭐⭐⭐ moderate
🕐 40 mins
🕐 1 hr 10 mins

🍳 **COOK'S TIP**

To make preserved lemons, cut enough lemons to fill a preserving jar into fourths lengthwise without cutting all the way through. Pack ¼ cup sea salt. Add the juice of 1 lemon and top up with water to cover. Leave for 1 month.

This is an unusual stew of sardines cooked with baby onions, tomatoes, olives, raisins, Marsala, and toasted pine nuts.

Stewed Sardines

1 Put the raisins into a small bowl and pour over the Marsala. Let soak for about 1 hour until the raisins are plump. Strain, reserving both the Marsala and the raisins.

2 Heat the olive oil in a large pan over low heat. Add the onions and cook for 15 minutes until golden and tender. Add the garlic and sage and cook for another 1 minute. Add the tomatoes and cook for another 2–3 minutes, then add the bouillon, vinegar, and reserved Marsala. Bring to a boil, cover and let simmer for 25 minutes.

3 Add the sardines to the stew and let simmer gently for 2–3 minutes before adding the raisins, olives, and pine nuts. Let simmer for a final 2–3 minutes until the fish are cooked. Add the parsley and transfer to 4 warmed serving plates. Garnish with lemon slices and serve immediately.

SERVES **4**

¾ cup raisins
3 tbsp Marsala
4 tbsp olive oil
8 oz/225 g baby onions, halved if large
2 garlic cloves, chopped
1 tbsp chopped fresh sage
4 large tomatoes, peeled and chopped
⅔ cup fish or vegetable bouillon
2 tbsp balsamic vinegar
1 lb/450 g fresh sardines, cleaned
¼ cup pitted black olives
1 oz/25 g pine nuts, toasted
2 tbsp chopped fresh parsley
lemon slices, to garnish

NUTRITION
Calories *412*; Sugars *14 g*; Protein *26 g*;
Carbohydrate *15 g*; Fat *27 g*; Saturates *5 g*

    easy

🕐   1 hr 15 mins

🕐   50 mins

🧑‍🍳 **COOK'S TIP**
Substitute Home-Salted Cod (see page 69) or smoked cod for the sardines.

This is a typical Thai curry, made with a paste of chiles and spices and a sauce of coconut milk. If you have access to a Thai supplier, buy ready-made curry paste as the Thais do.

Red Shrimp Curry

SERVES 4

2 tbsp vegetable oil
1 garlic clove, finely chopped
scant 1 cup coconut milk
2 tbsp Thai fish sauce
1 tsp sugar
12 large raw shrimp, peeled and deveined
2 kaffir lime leaves, shredded finely
1 fresh red chile, seeded and finely sliced
10 leaves Thai basil, if available,
    plus extra to garnish

red curry paste

3 dried long red chilies
½ tsp ground coriander
¼ tsp ground cumin
½ tsp pepper
2 garlic cloves, chopped
2 lemon grass stalks, chopped
1 kaffir lime leaf, chopped finely
1 tsp freshly grated gingerroot or galangal
1 tsp shrimp paste, optional
½ tsp salt

NUTRITION
Calories *149*; Sugars *4 g*; Protein *15 g*;
Carbohydrate *6 g*; Fat *7 g*; Saturates *1 g*

  easy

  15 mins

  10 mins

1 To make the red curry paste, put all the ingredients into a blender or spice grinder and process to a smooth paste, adding a little water, if necessary. Alternatively, pound the ingredients using a pestle and mortar. Transfer to a bowl and set aside.

2 Heat the vegetable oil in a preheated wok or large skillet over medium heat until almost smoking. Add the garlic and stir-fry until golden. Add 1 tablespoon of the curry paste and cook for another 1 minute. Add half the coconut milk, the Thai fish sauce, and the sugar. Stir well. The mixture should thicken slightly.

3 Add the shrimp and let simmer for 3–4 minutes until they turn pink. Add the remaining coconut milk, lime leaves and chile. Cook for another 2–3 minutes until the shrimp are just tender.

4 Add the basil leaves, stir until wilted and transfer to a large serving dish. Garnish with Thai basil and serve immediately.

COOK'S TIP

This recipe makes a little more curry paste than you need, but the paste keeps well. Stir a little into canned tuna with some chopped scallion, lime juice, and pinto beans for a delicious sandwich filling.

The best way to approach this recipe is to prepare everything beforehand—including measuring out the spices. The cooking time is then very quick.

Curried Shrimp *with* Zucchini

1 Cut the zucchini into small batons, then put into a strainer and sprinkle with a little of the salt. Set aside for 30 minutes. Rinse, drain, and pat dry with paper towels. Spread the shrimp on paper towels to drain.

2 Heat the vegetable oil in a preheated wok or skillet over high heat. Add the garlic. As soon as it starts to brown, add the zucchini, cilantro, green chile, turmeric, cumin, cayenne, tomatoes, ginger, lemon juice, and remaining salt. Stir well and bring to a boil.

3 Reduce the heat to low, cover and let simmer over low heat for 5 minutes. Uncover and add the shrimp.

4 Increase the heat to high and let simmer for about 5 minutes to reduce the liquid to a thick sauce. Transfer to 4 large, warmed serving plates and garnish with lime slices. Serve immediately, with steamed basmati rice.

SERVES 4

12 oz small zucchini
1 tsp salt
1 lb/450 g cooked jumbo shrimp
5 tbsp vegetable oil
4 garlic cloves, chopped finely
5 tbsp chopped fresh cilantro
1 fresh green chile, seeded
    and finely chopped
1/2 tsp ground turmeric
1 1/2 tsp ground cumin
pinch of cayenne pepper
7 oz/200 g canned chopped tomatoes
1 tsp freshly grated gingerroot
1 tbsp lemon juice
lime slices, to garnish
steamed basmati rice, to serve

NUTRITION
Calories *272*; Sugars *5 g*; Protein *29 g*;
Carbohydrate *5 g*; Fat *15 g*; Saturates *2 g*

easy

40 mins

15 mins

 COOK'S TIP

If you can't find cooked jumbo shrimp for this recipe, use smaller cooked shrimp instead, but these release quite a lot of liquid so you may need to increase the final simmering time to thicken the sauce.

Salads *and* Summer Dishes

Fish is the perfect supper ingredient if you are short of time because it cooks so quickly. It can be marinated and simply broiled or barbecued to make the basis of a range of salads, both warm and cold.

This chapter contains a variety of simple recipes which will taste as if you have spent hours preparing them. There are substantial main course salads, like Tuna Bean Salad, Moroccan Couscous Salad, and Caesar Salad. Quick meals include Salmon Frittata, and Tuna Fish Cakes. There are lots of barbecue ideas as well, including Barbecued Monkfish, Barbecued Scallops, and Mixed Seafood Brochettes.

Caesar salad was the invention of a chef at a large hotel in Tijuana in Mexico. This dish has rightly earned an international reputation.

Caesar Salad

SERVES 4

1 large romaine lettuce or
  2 hearts of romaine
4 canned anchovy fillets, drained
  and halved lengthwise
fresh Parmesan shavings, to garnish

dressing

2 garlic cloves, crushed
1½ tsp Dijon mustard
1 tsp Worcestershire sauce
4 canned anchovy fillets in olive oil,
  drained and chopped
1 egg yolk
1 tbsp lemon juice
⅔ cup olive oil
4 tbsp freshly grated Parmesan cheese
salt and pepper

croutons

4 thick slices day-old bread
2 tbsp olive oil
1 garlic clove, minced

NUTRITION

Calories *589*; Sugars *3 g*; Protein *11 g*;
Carbohydrate *24 g*; Fat *50 g*; Saturates *9 g*

 easy

 25 mins

🕐 15–20 mins

1 To make the dressing, put the garlic, mustard, Worcestershire sauce, anchovies, egg yolk, lemon juice and seasoning into a food processor or blender and process for 30 seconds, until foaming. Keeping the machine running, gradually add the olive oil, drop by drop until the mixture starts to thicken. Continue to add the olive oil until all the oil is incorporated. Transfer to a bowl and add a little hot water if the dressing is too thick. Stir in the Parmesan cheese. Season to taste with salt and pepper, if necessary, and let chill in the refrigerator until required.

2 To make the croutons, cut the bread into ½-inch/1-cm cubes. Put the olive oil and garlic into a bowl, add the bread cubes and toss well. Transfer to a baking sheet in a single layer and bake in a preheated oven, 350°F/190°C, for 15–20 minutes, stirring occasionally, until the croutons are browned and crisp. Remove from the oven and let cool.

3 Separate the romaine lettuce into individual leaves and wash. Tear into pieces and spin dry in a salad spinner. Alternatively, dry the leaves on clean paper towels. (Excess moisture will dilute the dressing and make the salad taste watery.) Transfer to a plastic bag and let chill until required.

4 To assemble the salad, put the lettuce pieces into a large serving bowl. Add the dressing and toss thoroughly until all the leaves are coated. Top with the halved anchovies, croutons, and Parmesan shavings. Serve while still hot.

Couscous is a type of fine semolina made from wheat. Traditionally it is steamed over a stew in a couscousier, which is a large pot with a steamer attachment that sits on the top. Nowadays, you can use precooked to save time.

Moroccan Couscous Salad

1 Cook the couscous according to the package instructions, omitting any butter recommended. Transfer to a large bowl and set aside.

2 Heat a small skillet over high heat. Add the cinnamon stick, coriander seeds, and cumin seeds and cook until the seeds start to pop and smell fragrant. Remove from the heat and pour the seeds into a mortar. Grind with a pestle to a fine powder. Alternatively, grind in a spice grinder. Set aside.

3 Heat the olive oil in a clean skillet over low heat. Add the onion and cook for 7–8 minutes until softened and lightly browned. Add the garlic and cook for another 1 minute. Stir in the roasted and ground spices, turmeric, and cayenne and cook for another 1 minute. Remove from the heat and stir in the lemon juice. Add this mixture to the couscous and mix well, ensuring that all of the grains are coated.

4 Add the golden raisins, tomatoes, cucumber, scallions, tuna, and chopped cilantro. Season to taste with salt and pepper and mix together. Let cool completely and serve at room temperature.

SERVES 4

1 cup couscous
1 cinnamon stick, about 2 inches/5 cm
2 tsp coriander seeds
1 tsp cumin seeds
2 tbsp olive oil
1 small onion, chopped finely
2 garlic cloves, chopped finely
½ tsp ground turmeric
pinch of cayenne pepper
1 tbsp lemon juice
¼ cup golden raisins
3 ripe plum tomatoes, chopped
½ cucumber, chopped
4 scallions, sliced
7 oz/200 g canned tuna in olive oil, drained and flaked
3 tbsp chopped fresh cilantro
salt and pepper

NUTRITION
Calories *329*; Sugars *12 g*; Protein *19 g*; Carbohydrate *42 g*; Fat *11 g*; Saturates *2 g*

easy

40 mins

20 mins

🍳 COOK'S TIP
Freshly cooked flaked salmon or tuna would work very well in this salad.

This is a classic version of
the French Salade Niçoise.
It is a substantial salad,
suitable for a lunch or light
summer meal.

Tuna Niçoise Salad

SERVES 4

4 eggs
1 lb/450 g new potatoes
1 cup dwarf green beans,
    trimmed and halved
6 oz/175 g tuna steaks
6 tbsp olive oil, plus extra for brushing
1 garlic clove, crushed
1½ tsp Dijon mustard
2 tsp lemon juice
2 tbsp chopped fresh basil
2 baby lettuces
1½ cups cherry tomatoes, halved
2 cups cucumber, peeled, cut in half,
    and sliced
½ cup pitted black olives
1¾ oz/50 g canned anchovy fillets
    in oil, drained
salt and pepper

NUTRITION

Calories *109*; Sugars *1.1 g*; Protein *7.2 g*;
Carbohydrate *4.8 g*; Fat *7 g*; Saturates *1.2 g*

easy

10 mins

20 mins

1 Bring a small pan of water to a boil over medium heat Add the eggs and
cook for 7–9 minutes from when the water returns to a boil—7 minutes for
a slightly soft center, 9 minutes for a firm center. Drain and refresh under
cold running water. Set aside.

2 Bring a large pan of lightly salted water to a boil over medium heat. Add the
potatoes and cook for 10–12 minutes until tender. Add the beans 3 minutes
before the end of the cooking time. Drain both vegetables well and refresh
under cold running water. Drain well.

3 Wash the tuna steaks under cold running water and pat dry with paper
towels. Brush with a little olive oil and season to taste with salt and pepper.
Cook on a preheated ridged griddle for 2–3 minutes on each side, until just
tender, but still slightly pink in the center. Let rest.

4 Whisk the garlic, mustard, lemon juice, basil and seasoning together. Whisk
in the olive oil.

5 To assemble the salad, break apart the lettuces and tear into large pieces.
Divide among 4 large serving plates. Add the potatoes and beans, tomatoes,
cucumber, and olives. Toss lightly together. Shell the eggs and cut into
fourths lengthwise. Arrange these on top of the salad. Sprinkle over the
drained anchovies.

6 Flake the tuna steaks and arrange on the salads. Pour over the dressing and
serve immediately.

Don't panic if you forget to soak the dried beans overnight. Place them in a saucepan with plenty of water, bring to a boil, turn off the heat and leave to soak, covered, for at least 2 hours before cooking.

Tuna Bean Salad

1 Soak the navy beans for 8 hours or overnight in at least twice their volume of cold water.

2 When you're ready to cook, drain the beans and place in a pan with twice their volume of fresh water. Bring slowly to a boil over medium heat, skimming off any froth that rises to the surface with a draining spoon. Boil the beans rapidly for 10 minutes, then reduce the heat and let simmer for another $1\frac{1}{4}$–$1\frac{1}{2}$ hours until the beans are tender.

3 Meanwhile, mix the lemon juice, olive oil, garlic, and seasoning together. Drain the beans thoroughly and mix together with the olive oil mixture, onion, and parsley. Season to taste with salt and pepper and set aside.

4 Wash the tuna steaks under cold running water and pat dry with paper towels. Brush lightly with olive oil and season to taste with salt and pepper. Cook on a preheated ridged griddle for 2 minutes on each side until just pink in the center.

5 Divide the bean salad among 4 serving plates. Top each with a tuna steak. Garnish with a few sprigs of fresh parsley and lemon wedges and serve.

SERVES 4

1 cup dried navy beans
1 tbsp lemon juice
5 tbsp extra virgin olive oil,
    plus extra for brushing
1 garlic clove, chopped finely
1 small red onion, sliced very finely (optional)
1 tbsp chopped fresh parsley
6 oz/175 g tuna steaks
salt and pepper

to garnish
fresh parsley sprigs
lemon wedges

NUTRITION
Calories *529*; Sugars *3 g*; Protein *54 g*;
Carbohydrate *29 g*; Fat *23 g*; Saturates *4 g*

⭐⭐   easy
     8 hr 15 mins
     1 hr 30 mins

(👨‍🍳) **COOK'S TIP**

You could use canned navy beans instead of dried. Reheat according to the instructions on the can, drain and toss with the dressing as above.

A colorful, refreshing first course that is perfect to make for a special summer lunch or dinner. The dressing can be made in advance and spooned over just before serving.

Warm Tuna Salad

SERVES 4

½ cup Chinese cabbage, shredded
3 tbsp Chinese rice wine
2 tbsp Thai fish sauce
1 tbsp finely shredded fresh gingerroot
1 garlic clove, chopped finely
½ small bird's-eye red chile, chopped finely
2 tsp light brown sugar
2 tbsp lime juice
14 oz/400 g fresh tuna steak
1 tbsp corn oil, for brushing
1 cup cherry tomatoes
chopped fresh mint leaves and fresh mint sprigs, to garnish

1 Place a small pile of shredded Chinese cabbage on a large serving plate. Place the Chinese rice wine, Thai fish sauce, ginger, garlic, chile, brown sugar, and 1 tablespoon of lime juice in a jar and shake well to mix.

2 Cut the tuna steaks into strips of an even thickness, then sprinkle with the remaining lime juice.

3 Brush a wide skillet or preheated ridged griddle with the corn oil and heat until very hot. Arrange the tuna strips in the skillet and cook until just firm and light golden, turning them over once. Remove and set aside.

4 Add the tomatoes to the skillet and cook over high heat until lightly browned. Spoon the tuna and tomatoes over the Chinese cabbage and spoon over the dressing. Sprinkle with chopped fresh mint and a few sprigs of fresh mint and serve warm.

NUTRITION
Calories 177; Sugars 4 g; Protein 13 g;
Carbohydrate 6 g; Fat 6 g; Saturates 1 g

easy

15 mins

8 mins

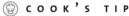 **COOK'S TIP**

You can make a quick version of this dish using canned tuna. Just drain and flake the tuna, omit Steps 2 and 3, and continue as in the recipe above.

This unusual seafood dish with a sweet lime dressing can be either an appetizer or doubled up for a buffet-style main dish. It is also the perfect dish to prepare for a crowd if you're entertaining.

Sweet-*and*-Sour Seafood

1 Clean the mussels by scrubbing or scraping the shells and pulling out any beards that are attached to them. Discard any with broken shells or any that refuse to close when tapped. Put them into a large pan with just the water that clings to their shells and cook, covered, over high heat for 3–4 minutes, shaking the pan occasionally, until the mussels are opened. Discard any that remain closed. Strain the mussels, reserving the liquid in the pan.

2 Separate the corals from the scallops and cut the whites in half horizontally. Cut the tentacles from the squid and slice the body cavities into rings.

3 Add the shallots to the liquid in the pan and let simmer over high heat until the liquid is reduced to about 3 tablespoons. Add the scallops, squid, and jumbo shrimp and stir for 2–3 minutes until cooked. Remove the pan from the heat and spoon into a wide bowl.

4 Cut the cucumber and carrot in half lengthwise, then slice thinly on a diagonal angle to make long, pointed slices. Toss with the Chinese cabbage.

5 To make the dressing, place all the ingredients in a screw-top jar and shake well until blended. Season to taste with salt and pepper.

6 Toss the vegetables and seafood together. Spoon the dressing over the vegetables and seafood and serve immediately.

SERVES 4

18 live mussels in shell
6 large scallops
7 oz/200 g baby squid, cleaned
2 shallots, chopped finely
6 raw jumbo shrimp, peeled and deveined
¼ cucumber
1 carrot, peeled
¼ head Chinese cabbage, shredded

dressing
4 tbsp lime juice
2 garlic cloves, chopped finely
2 tbsp Thai fish sauce
1 tsp sesame oil
1 tbsp light brown sugar
2 tbsp chopped fresh mint
¼ tsp pepper
salt

NUTRITION
Calories 97; Sugars 5 g; Protein 13 g;
Carbohydrate 8 g; Fat 2 g; Saturates 0 g

 moderate

20 mins

10 mins

Use whatever shellfish is available. For best results, this salad should be served chilled.

Thai Seafood Salad

S E R V E S 4

1 lb/450 g live mussels
8 raw jumbo shrimp
12 oz/350 g squid, cleaned and sliced widthwise into rings
4 oz/115 g cooked peeled shrimp
½ red onion, sliced finely
½ red bell pepper, seeded and finely sliced
1 cup bean sprouts
2 cups shredded bok choi

dressing
1 garlic clove, crushed
1 tsp grated fresh gingerroot
1 red chile, seeded and finely chopped
2 tbsp chopped fresh cilantro
1 tbsp lime juice
1 tsp finely grated lime rind
1 tbsp light soy sauce
5 tbsp corn or peanut oil
2 tsp sesame oil
4 tbsp cold water
salt and pepper

N U T R I T I O N
Calories *310*; Sugars *4 g*; Protein *30 g*;
Carbohydrate *7 g*; Fat *18 g*; Saturates *3 g*

 easy

 1 hr 15 mins

10 mins

1 Clean the mussels by scrubbing or scraping the shells and removing any beards that are attached to them. Place in a large pan with just the water that clings to their shells and cook, covered, over high heat for 3–4 minutes, shaking the pan occasionally, until all the mussels have opened. Discard any that remain closed. Strain the mussels, reserving the liquid in the pan, and refresh the mussels under cold running water. Drain again and set aside.

2 Bring the reserved liquid to a boil over medium heat. Add the jumbo shrimp and let simmer for 5 minutes. Add the squid and cook for another 2 minutes until both the shrimp and squid are cooked through. Remove them with a draining spoon and plunge immediately into a large bowl of cold water. Reserve the liquid in the pan. Drain the shrimp and squid again.

3 Remove the mussels from their shells and put into a bowl with the jumbo shrimp, squid, and cooked peeled shrimp. Let chill for 1 hour.

4 To make the dressing, put all the ingredients, except the oils, into a blender or spice grinder and blend to a smooth paste. Add the oils, reserved poaching liquid, seasoning to taste and the water. Process until blended.

5 Just before serving, mix the onion, red bell pepper, bean sprouts, and bok choi in a bowl and toss with 2–3 tablespoons of the dressing. Arrange the vegetables on a large serving plate or in a bowl. Toss the remaining dressing with the seafood to coat and add to the vegetables. Serve immediately.

Noodles and bean sprouts form the basis of this refreshing salad, which combines the flavors of fruit and shrimp.

Chinese Shrimp Salad

1 Place the egg noodles in a large bowl and pour over enough boiling water to cover. Let stand for 10 minutes.

2 Drain the noodles thoroughly and pat dry with paper towels.

3 Heat the corn oil in a large preheated wok or skillet over medium heat. Add the noodles and cook for 5 minutes, tossing frequently.

4 Remove the wok from the heat and add the sesame oil, sesame seeds, and bean sprouts, tossing to mix well.

5 Mix the sliced mango, scallions, radishes, and shrimp together in a separate bowl. Stir in the soy sauce and sherry and mix until thoroughly blended.

6 Toss the shrimp mixture with the noodles and transfer to a serving dish. Alternatively, arrange the noodles around the edge of a serving plate and pile the shrimp mixture into the center. Serve immediately as this salad is best eaten warm.

SERVES 4

9 oz/250 g fine egg noodles
3 tbsp corn oil
1 tbsp sesame oil
1 tbsp sesame seeds
1½ cups bean sprouts
1 ripe mango, sliced
6 scallions, sliced
2¾ oz/75 g radishes, sliced
12 oz/350 g cooked peeled shrimp
2 tbsp light soy sauce
1 tbsp sherry

NUTRITION
Calories 359; Sugars 4 g; Protein 31 g;
Carbohydrate 25 g; Fat 15 g; Saturates 2 g

⭐⭐ easy
🕐 15 mins
🕐 5 mins

 COOK'S TIP

If fresh ripe mango is unavailable, use canned mango slices, rinsed and drained, instead.

This salad makes a filling main course or would serve six as an appetizer. Fresh skate should have a faint smell of ammonia; if the smell is very strong, do not use the fish.

Skate *and* Spinach Salad

S E R V E S   4

1 lb 9 oz/700 g skate wings, trimmed
2 fresh rosemary sprigs
1 bay leaf
1 tbsp black peppercorns
1 lemon, cut into fourths
1 lb/450 g baby spinach leaves
1 tbsp olive oil
1 small red onion, sliced thinly
2 garlic cloves, crushed
½ tsp chili flakes
½ cup pine nuts, toasted lightly
½ cup raisins
1 tbsp light brown sugar
2 tbsp chopped fresh parsley

N U T R I T I O N
Calories 316; Sugars 18 g; Protein 32 g;
Carbohydrate 18 g; Fat 13 g; Saturates 1 g

easy

30 mins

15 mins

1 Put the skate wings into a pan with the rosemary, bay leaf, peppercorns, and lemon fourths. Cover with cold water and bring to a boil over medium heat. Let simmer, covered, for 4–5 minutes until the flesh starts to come away from the cartilage. Remove from the heat and let stand for 15 minutes.

2 Lift the fish from the poaching water and remove the flesh from the fish in shreds. Set aside.

3 Meanwhile, put the spinach in a clean pan and cook with just the water that clings to the leaves after washing, over high heat for 30 seconds until just wilted. Drain, then refresh under cold running water and drain well again. Squeeze out any excess water and set aside.

4 Heat the olive oil in a large, deep skillet over low heat. Add the red onion and cook for 3–4 minutes until softened, but not browned. Add the garlic, chili flakes, pine nuts, raisins, and sugar and cook for 1–2 minutes, then add the spinach, and toss for 1 minute until heated through.

5 Gently fold in the skate and cook for another 1 minute. Season well with salt and pepper.

6 Divide the salad among 4 serving plates and sprinkle with the chopped parsley. Serve immediately.

A colorful combination of cooked mussels tossed together with charbroiled red bell peppers, radicchio, and arugula, and a tasty lemon and chive dressing. It makes a delicious main meal.

Mussel *and* Red Bell Pepper Salad

1 Halve and seed the bell peppers and place them skin side up on a broiler rack. Cook under a preheated broiler for 8–10 minutes until the skin is charred and blistered and the flesh is soft. Let cool for 10 minutes, then peel off the skin.

2 Slice the bell pepper flesh into thin strips and place in a bowl. Gently mix in the shelled mussels and set aside.

3 To make the dressing, mix all of the ingredients in a small bowl until well blended. Mix into the bell pepper and mussel mixture until coated.

4 Remove the central core of the radicchio and shred the leaves. Place in a serving bowl with the arugula and toss together.

5 Pile the mussel mixture into the center of the leaves and arrange the large mussels around the edge of the dish. Garnish with strips of lemon rind and serve immediately with crusty bread.

SERVES 4

2 large red bell peppers
12oz/350 g cooked shelled mussels, thawed
   if frozen
1 head of radicchio
1 oz/25 g arugula
8 cooked New Zealand mussels
   in their shells
strips of lemon rind, to garnish
crusty bread, to serve

dressing
1 tbsp olive oil
1 tbsp lemon juice
1 tsp finely grated lemon rind
2 tsp honey
1 tsp French mustard
1 tbsp chopped fresh chives
salt and pepper

NUTRITION
Calories *180*; Sugars *10 g*; Protein *18 g*;
Carbohydrate *14 g*; Fat *6 g*; Saturates *1 g*

 easy
30 mins
 10 mins

🍲 **COOK'S TIP**

Replace the shelled mussels with peeled shrimp and the New Zealand mussels with large crevettes, if you prefer. Lime could be used instead of lemon for a different citrus flavor.

Try to get small red mullet for this dish. If you can only get larger fish, serve one to each person and then increase the cooking time accordingly.

Broiled Red Mullet

SERVES 4

1 lemon, sliced thinly
2 garlic cloves, minced
4 fresh flatleaf parsley sprigs
4 fresh thyme sprigs
8 fresh sage leaves
2 large shallots, sliced
8 small red mullet, cleaned
8 slices prosciutto
salt and pepper

sauté potatoes and shallots
4 tbsp olive oil
2 lb/900 g potatoes, peeled and diced
8 whole garlic cloves, unpeeled
12 small whole shallots

dressing
4 tbsp olive oil
1 tbsp lemon juice
1 tbsp chopped fresh flatleaf parsley
1 tbsp chopped fresh chives

1 For the sauté potatoes and shallots, heat the olive oil in a large skillet over medium heat. Add the potatoes, garlic cloves, and shallots and cook gently, stirring regularly, for 12–15 minutes until golden, crisp, and tender.

2 Meanwhile, divide the lemon slices, halved if necessary, garlic, parsley, thyme, sage, and shallots among the cavities of the fish. Season well with salt and pepper. Wrap a slice of prosciutto around each fish. Secure with a toothpick.

3 Arrange the fish on a broiler pan and cook under a preheated hot broiler for 5–6 minutes on each side until tender.

4 To make the dressing, mix the olive oil and lemon juice, parsley, and chives together in a small bowl. Season to taste with salt and pepper.

5 Divide the potatoes and shallots among 4 serving plates and top each with the fish. Drizzle around the dressing and serve immediately.

NUTRITION

Calories *111*; Sugars *0.8 g*; Protein *10.2 g*;
Carbohydrate *6 g*; Fat *5 g*; Saturates *1 g*

moderate

10 mins

20 mins

Liven up firm steaks of white fish with a spicy, colorful relish. Use red onions for a slightly sweeter flavor.

Pan-Seared Halibut

1 To make the relish, peel and thinly shred the onions and shallots. Place in a small bowl and toss in the lemon juice.

2 Heat the olive oil for the relish in a pan over low heat. Add the onions and shallots and cook for 3–4 minutes until just softened.

3 Add the vinegar and sugar and continue to cook for another 2 minutes over high heat. Pour in the bouillon and season well with salt and pepper. Bring to a boil and let simmer gently for another 8–9 minutes until the sauce has thickened and is slightly reduced.

4 Brush a non-stick, ridged griddle or skillet with olive oil and heat over medium–high until hot. Press the fish steaks into the pan to seal, reduce the heat and cook for 4 minutes. Turn the fish over and cook for 4–5 minutes until cooked through. Drain on paper towels and keep warm.

5 Stir the cornstarch paste into the onion relish and heat through, stirring, until thickened. Season to taste with salt and pepper.

6 Pile the relish onto 4 warmed serving plates and place a halibut steak on top of each. Garnish with chopped chives and serve.

SERVES 4

1 tsp olive oil
4 halibut steaks, skinned, about
   6 oz/175 g each
$\frac{1}{2}$ tsp cornstarch mixed with
   2 tsp cold water
salt and pepper
2 tbsp chopped fresh chives, to garnish

red onion relish
2 tsp olive oil
2 medium red onions
6 shallots
1 tbsp lemon juice
2 tbsp red wine vinegar
2 tsp superfine sugar
$\frac{2}{3}$ cup Fresh Fish Bouillon (see page 14)

NUTRITION
Calories 197; Sugars 1 g; Protein 31 g;
Carbohydrate 2 g; Fat 7 g; Saturates 1 g

  moderate
55 mins
30 mins

🍳 **COOK'S TIP**

If raw onions make your eyes water, try peeling them under cold running water. Alternatively, stand or sit well back from the onion so that your face isn't directly over it.

This is a wonderful dish to serve as part of a buffet lunch or supper and can be eaten hot or cold.

Baked Salmon

SERVES 8–10

6 lb 8 oz/3 kg salmon filleted
8 tbsp chopped mixed herbs
2 tbsp green peppercorns in brine, drained
1 tsp finely grated lime rind
6 tbsp dry vermouth or dry white wine
salt and pepper
fresh parsley sprigs, to garnish

red bell pepper relish
½ cup white wine vinegar
¼ cups light olive oil
1–2 tsp chili sauce, to taste
6 scallions, sliced finely
1 orange or red bell pepper, seeded, and
 finely diced
1 tbsp chopped fresh flatleaf parsley
2 tbsp chopped fresh chives

caper mayonnaise
1½ cups good-quality mayonnaise
3 tbsp chopped capers
3 tbsp finely chopped gherkins
2 tbsp chopped fresh flatleaf parsley
1 tbsp Dijon mustard

NUTRITION

Calories *892*; Sugars *2 g*; Protein *41 g*;
Carbohydrate *2 g*; Fat *79 g*; Saturates *12 g*

easy

30 mins

12 mins

1 Wash the salmon fillets under cold running water and pat dry with paper towels. Place 1 fillet, skin side down, on a large sheet of oiled foil. Mix together the herbs, peppercorns, and lime rind and spread over the top. Season well with salt and pepper and lay the second fillet on top, skin side up. Drizzle over the vermouth or white wine. Wrap the foil over the salmon, twisting well to make a loose but tightly sealed parcel.

2 Transfer the foil parcel to a large baking sheet and bake in a preheated oven, at 250°F/120°C, for 1½ hours until tender. Remove from the oven and let rest for 20 minutes before serving.

3 Meanwhile, make the red bell pepper relish. Whisk the vinegar, olive oil, and chile sauce together in a small bowl. Add the scallions, red bell pepper, parsley, and chives. Season to taste with salt and pepper and set aside.

4 To make the caper and gherkin mayonnaise, mix all the ingredients together in a small bowl and set aside.

5 Unwrap the cooked salmon and slice thickly. Arrange the slices on a large serving platter and garnish with fresh parsley sprigs. Serve with the red bell pepper relish and caper and gherkin mayonnaise.

Monkfish cooks very well on a barbecue because it is a firm-fleshed fish.

Barbecued Monkfish

1   Mix the olive oil, lime rind, Thai fish sauce, garlic, ginger, and basil together. Season to taste with salt and pepper and set aside.

2   Wash the fish under cold running water and pat dry with paper towels. Add to the marinade and mix well. Cover and let marinate in the refrigerator for 2 hours, stirring occasionally.

3   If you are using bamboo skewers, soak them in cold water for 30 minutes. Lift the monkfish pieces from the marinade and thread them onto the skewers, alternating with the lime wedges.

4   Transfer the skewers either to a lit barbecue or to a preheated ridged griddle and cook for 5–6 minutes, turning regularly, until the fish is tender. Pile freshly cooked noodles onto 4 large, warmed serving plates and put the monkfish kabobs on top. Garnish with a few fresh basil leaves and serve.

SERVES 4

4 tbsp olive oil
grated rind of 1 lime
2 tsp Thai fish sauce
2 garlic cloves, crushed
1 tsp grated fresh gingerroot
2 tbsp chopped fresh basil
1 lb 9 oz/700 g monkfish fillet,
    cut into chunks
2 limes, cut into 6 wedges
salt and pepper
fresh basil leaves, to garnish
freshly cooked noodles, to serve

NUTRITION
Calories *219*; Sugars *2 g*; Protein *41 g*;
Carbohydrate *2 g*; Fat *79 g*; Saturates *12 g*

⭐⭐   easy

🕑   2 hrs 10 mins

🕐   6 mins

 COOK'S TIP

You could use any type of white fish for this recipe, but sprinkle the pieces with salt and let stand for 2 hours to firm the flesh, before rinsing, drying, and then adding to the marinade.

Tuna has a firm flesh, which is ideal for barbecuing, but it can be a little dry unless it is marinated first.

Charred Tuna Steaks

S E R V E S   4

4 tuna steaks
3 tbsp soy sauce
1 tbsp Worcestershire sauce
1 tsp wholegrain mustard
1 tsp superfine sugar
1 tbsp corn oil
salad greens, to serve

to garnish
fresh flatleaf parsley sprigs
lemon wedges

1 Place the tuna steaks in a large, shallow dish.

2 Mix the soy sauce, Worcestershire sauce, mustard, sugar, and corn oil together in a small bowl. Pour the marinade over the tuna steaks.

3 Gently turn the tuna steaks, using your fingers or a fork, so that they are well coated with the marinade.

4 Cover with plastic wrap and let the tuna steaks marinate in the refrigerator for at least 30 minutes or preferably 2 hours.

5 Transfer the marinated fish to a lit barbecue and cook over hot coals for 10–15 minutes, turning once. Baste frequently with any of the marinade that is left in the dish.

6 Transfer the tuna to 4 large serving plates, garnish with a few fresh sprigs of parsley and lemon wedges, and serve with fresh salad greens.

N U T R I T I O N
Calories *510*; Sugars *38 g*; Protein *33 g*;
Carbohydrate *44 g*; Fat *24 g*; Saturates *11 g*

 moderate

 2 hrs

15 mins

 **C O O K ' S   T I P**

If a marinade contains soy sauce, the marinating time should be limited to 2 hours. If marinated for too long, the fish will dry out and become tough.

The fish is "blackened" because the spicy marinade that is used to coat it chars slightly as it cooks. Choose a fish with a firm texture, such as hake or halibut, for this dish.

Blackened Fish

1 Wash the fish under cold running water and pat dry with paper towels.

2 Mix the paprika, thyme, cayenne pepper, black and white peppers, salt, and allspice together in a shallow dish.

3 Place the butter and oil in a pan and heat over low heat, stirring occasionally, until the butter melts.

4 Brush the butter mixture liberally all over the fish steaks, on both sides.

5 Dip the fish into the spicy mix until well coated on both sides.

6 Transfer the fish to a lit barbecue and cook over hot coals for 10 minutes on each side, turning it over once. Continue to baste the fish with the remaining butter mixture during the cooking time. Transfer the fish to 4 large serving plates and serve with mixed salad greens.

SERVES 4

4 white fish steaks
1 tbsp paprika
1 tsp dried thyme
1 tsp cayenne pepper
1 tsp pepper
½ tsp freshly ground white pepper
½ tsp salt
¼ tsp ground allspice
4 tbsp unsalted butter
3 tbsp corn oil
mixed salad greens, to serve

NUTRITION
Calories 370; Sugars 0 g; Protein 27 g;
Carbohydrate 52 g; Fat 8 g; Saturates 1 q

 moderate

5–10 mins

20 mins

COOK'S TIP

A whole fish—red mullet, for example—rather than steaks is also delicious cooked this way. The spicy seasoning can also be used to coat chicken portions, if you prefer.

The Japanese sauce used here combines very well with the salmon, although it is usually served with chicken.

Salmon Yakitori

SERVES 4

12 oz/350 g chunky salmon fillet
8 baby leeks
fresh herbs, to garnish

yakitori sauce
5 tbsp light soy sauce
5 tbsp fish bouillon
2 tbsp superfine sugar
5 tbsp dry white wine
3 tbsp sweet sherry
1 garlic clove, crushed

NUTRITION
Calories *247*; Sugars *10 g*; Protein *19 g*;
Carbohydrate *12 g*; Fat *11 g*; Saturates *2 g*

⭐⭐   easy

🕐   20 mins

🕐   15 mins

1 Skin the salmon and cut the flesh into 2-inch/5-cm chunks. Trim the leeks and cut them into 2-inch/5-cm lengths.

2 Thread the salmon and leeks alternately onto 8 presoaked wooden skewers. Let chill in the refrigerator until required.

3 To make the sauce, place all of the ingredients in a small pan and heat gently over low heat, stirring, until the sugar dissolves. Bring to a boil, then reduce the heat, and let simmer for 2 minutes. Strain the sauce and let cool. Pour about one third of the sauce into a small dish and set aside to serve with the kabobs.

4 Brush plenty of the remaining sauce over the skewers and transfer the skewers to a lit barbecue. Cook over hot coals for about 10 minutes, turning once. Cook directly on a broiler rack or, if preferred, place a sheet of greased foil on the rack and cook the salmon on the foil. Baste the skewers frequently during cooking with the remaining sauce to prevent the fish and vegetables from drying out.

5 Transfer the kabobs to a large serving plate, garnish with fresh herbs and serve with the dish of reserved sauce for dipping.

🍳 **COOK'S TIP**

Soak wooden skewers in cold water for at least 30 minutes to prevent them burning during cooking. You can make the kabobs and sauce several hours ahead of time and keep in the refrigerator until required.

A delicious aromatic coating makes this dish rather special. Serve it with a crisp salad and lots of crusty bread, if desired.

Indonesian-Style Spicy Cod

1 Wash the cod steaks under cold running water and pat dry on paper towels.

2 Remove and discard the outer leaves from the lemongrass stalk and thinly slice the inner section.

3 Put the lemongrass, onion, garlic, chiles, ginger, and turmeric into a food processor and process until the ingredients are finely chopped. Season to taste with salt and pepper. Keeping the machine running, add the butter, coconut milk, and lemon juice and process until well blended.

4 Place the fish in a shallow, non-metallic dish. Pour the coconut mixture on top and turn the fish until well coated.

5 If you have one, place the fish steaks in a hinged basket, which will make them easier to turn. Transfer the fish steaks to a lit barbecue and cook over hot coals for 15 minutes or until the fish is cooked through, turning once. Transfer the fish steaks to 4 large serving plates, garnish with red chiles, if desired, and serve with mixed salad greens.

SERVES 4

4 cod steaks
1 lemongrass stalk
1 small red onion, chopped
3 garlic cloves, chopped
2 fresh red chiles, seeded and chopped
1 tsp grated fresh gingerroot
¼ tsp turmeric
2 tbsp butter, cut into small cubes
8 tbsp canned coconut milk
2 tbsp lemon juice
salt and pepper
fresh red chiles, to garnish (optional)
mixed salad greens, to serve

NUTRITION
Calories *146*; Sugars *2 g*; Protein *19 g*;
Carbohydrate *2 g*; Fat *7 g*; Saturates *4 g*

✪✪   easy
🕐   10 mins
🕐   15 mins

 COOK'S TIP

If you prefer a milder flavor, omit the chiles altogether. For a hotter flavor do not remove the seeds from the chiles.

This is the genuine article. A crunchy, deep golden batter surrounding perfectly cooked cod, served with golden crispy chips. If you've never had chips with mayonnaise, try them with this lovely mustardy version and you'll be converted.

Fish *and* Chips

SERVES 4

2 lb/900 g old potatoes
6 oz/175 g thick pieces cod fillet, preferably from the head end
2 cups vegetable oil, for deep-frying
salt and pepper

batter
½ oz/15 g fresh yeast
1¼ cups beer
2 cups all-purpose flour
2 tsp salt

mayonnaise
1 egg yolk
1 tsp wholegrain mustard
1 tbsp lemon juice
1 cup light olive oil
salt and pepper

to garnish
lemon wedges
fresh parsley sprigs

NUTRITION
Calories *584*; Sugars *0 g*; Protein *28 g*;
Carbohydrate *1 g*; Fat *48 g*; Saturates *7 g*

easy
1 hr 10 mins
30–35 mins

1 To make the batter, cream the yeast with a little of the beer to a smooth paste. Gradually stir in the rest of the beer. Strain the flour and salt into a bowl, make a well in the center and add the yeast mixture. Gradually whisk to a smooth batter. Cover and let stand at room temperature for 1 hour.

2 To make the mayonnaise, put the egg yolk, mustard, lemon juice, and seasoning into a food processor and process for 30 seconds until frothy. Gradually add the olive oil, drop by drop, until the mixture starts to thicken. Continue adding the olive oil in a slow, steady stream until all the oil is incorporated. Season to taste with salt and pepper, if necessary and add with a little hot water if the mixture is too thick. Let chill until required.

3 For the chips, cut the potatoes into chips about ½ inch/1 cm thick. Half fill a large pan with vegetable oil and heat to 275°F/140°C, or until a cube of bread browns in 1 minute. Add the chips in 2 batches and cook for 5 minutes, until cooked through, but not browned. Drain on paper towels and set aside.

4 Increase the heat to 325°F/160°C, or until a cube of bread browns in 45 seconds. Season the fish, then dip into the batter. Add 2 pieces at a time and cook for 7–8 minutes until golden brown and cooked through. Drain on paper towels and keep warm while you cook remaining fish.

5 Increase the heat to 375°F/190°C, or until a cube of bread browns in 30 seconds. Deep-fry the chips again, in 2 batches, for 2–3 minutes until crisp and golden. Drain on paper and sprinkle with salt. Serve the fish with the chips and mayonnaise, garnished with lemon wedges and parsley sprigs.

The Italian flat bread known as focaccia is what makes these battered haddock fingers taste so special.

Haddock Goujons

1 Put the focaccia into a food processor and process until fine crumbs form. Set aside. Slice the haddock fillet widthwise into fingers. Put the flour, egg, and bread crumbs into separate bowls.

2 Dip the haddock fingers into the flour, then the egg, and finally the bread crumbs to coat. Lay on a plate and let chill in the refrigerator for 30 minutes.

3 To make the tartar sauce, put the egg yolk, mustard, vinegar, and seasoning into a food processor and process for 30 seconds until frothy. Gradually add the olive oil, drop by drop, until the mixture starts to thicken. Continue adding the olive oil in a slow, steady stream until all the oil is incorporated. Transfer to a small bowl and stir in the olives, gherkins, capers, chives, and parsley. Season to taste with salt and pepper, if necessary and add a little hot water if the sauce is too thick.

4 Half fill a large pan with vegetable oil and heat to 375°F/190°C, or until a cube of bread browns in 30 seconds. Add the haddock goujons, in batches of 3 or 4 and cook for 3–4 minutes until the crumbs are browned and crisp and the fish is cooked. Drain on paper towels and keep warm while you cook the remaining fish.

5 Transfer the haddock goujons to 4 large serving plates and garnish with lemon wedges and a few sprigs of fresh parsley. Serve immediately.

SERVES 4

6 oz/175 g herb focaccia bread
1 lb 9 oz/700 g skinless, boneless
    haddock fillet
2–3 tbsp all-purpose flour
2 eggs, beaten lightly
2 cups vegetable oil, for deep-frying

tartar sauce
1 egg yolk
1 tsp Dijon mustard
2 tsp white wine vinegar
²⁄₃ cup light olive oil
1 tsp finely chopped green olives
1 tsp finely chopped gherkins
1 tsp finely chopped capers
2 tsp chopped fresh chives
2 tsp chopped fresh parsley
salt and pepper

to garnish
lemon wedges
fresh parsley sprigs

NUTRITION
Calories 762; Sugars 1 g; Protein 9 g;
Carbohydrate 4 g; Fat 1 g; Saturates 0.5 g

✪✪✪   moderate
          50 mins
🕐   15 mins

Salsa verde is a classic Italian sauce of herbs, garlic, and anchovies. The name simply means "green sauce," and the sauce is a perfect partner to fish.

Swordfish Steaks *in* Salsa Verde

SERVES 4

4 swordfish steaks, about 5½ oz/150 g each
4 tbsp olive oil
1 garlic clove, crushed
1 tsp lemon rind
lemon wedges, to garnish

salsa verde

1 cup flatleaf parsley leaves
½ cup mixed herbs, such as basil, mint, and chives
1 garlic clove, chopped
1 tbsp capers, drained and rinsed
1 tbsp green peppercorns in brine, drained
4 canned anchovy fillets in oil, drained and coarsely chopped
1 tsp Dijon mustard
½ cup extra virgin olive oil
salt and pepper

1 Wash the swordfish steaks under cold running water and pat dry with paper towels. Arrange in a non-metallic dish. Mix the olive oil, garlic, and lemon rind together. Pour over the swordfish steaks, cover and let marinate in the refrigerator for 2 hours.

2 To make the salsa verde, put the parsley leaves, mixed herbs, garlic, capers, green peppercorns, anchovies, mustard, and olive oil into a food processor or blender and process to a smooth paste, adding a little warm water, if necessary. Season to taste with salt and pepper and set aside.

3 Remove the swordfish steaks from the marinade. Transfer to a lit barbecue or preheated ridged griddle and cook for 2–3 minutes on each side until tender. Transfer the fish to 4 large serving plates, garnish with lemon wedges and serve immediately with the salsa verde.

NUTRITION
Calories *584*; Sugars *0 g*; Protein *28 g*;
Carbohydrate *1 g*; Fat *48 g*; Saturates *7 g*

easy

2 hrs 15 mins

4–6 mins

🍽 **COOK'S TIP**

Any firm-fleshed fish will do for this recipe. Try tuna or shark instead.

Fajitas are usually made with chicken or lamb but using a firm fish such as swordfish or tuna works very well.

Swordfish *or* Tuna Fajitas

1 Mix the olive oil, chili powder, cumin, cayenne, and garlic together in a large bowl. Cut the swordfish or tuna into chunks and mix with the marinade. Let stand for 1–2 hours.

2 Heat a large skillet over medium heat until hot. Add the fish and its marinade and cook for 2 minutes, stirring occasionally, until the fish starts to brown. Add the red bell pepper, yellow bell pepper, zucchini, and onion and continue cooking for another 5 minutes until the vegetables have softened, but still firm.

3 Meanwhile, warm the tortillas in a preheated oven or microwave according to the package instructions.

4 To make the guacamole, mash the avocado until fairly smooth, stir in the tomato, garlic, Tabasco, lemon juice, and seasoning to taste.

5 Add the lemon juice, cilantro, and salt and pepper to taste to the vegetable mix. Spoon some of the mixture down the center of the warmed tortilla. Top with guacamole and a spoonful of sour cream and roll up. Transfer to a large serving plate and garnish with a few sprigs of fresh cilantro to serve.

SERVES 4

3 tbsp olive oil
2 tsp chili powder
1 tsp ground cumin
pinch of cayenne pepper
1 garlic clove, crushed
2 lb/900 g swordfish or tuna
1 red and 1 yellow bell pepper, seeded
  and thinly sliced
2 zucchini, cut into batons
1 large onion, sliced thinly
12 soft flour tortillas
1 tbsp lemon juice
3 tbsp chopped fresh cilantro
salt and pepper
²⁄₃ cup sour cream, to serve

guacamole
1 large ripe avocado
1 tomato, peeled, seeded, and diced
1 garlic clove, crushed
dash of Tabasco sauce
2 tbsp lemon juice
salt and pepper

NUTRITION
Calories 766; Sugars 12 g; Protein 52 g;
Carbohydrate 63 g; Fat 36 g; Saturates 10 g

 easy

1 hr 15 mins

 7 mins

The marinade for this dish has a distinctly Japanese flavor. Its subtle taste goes well with any white fish.

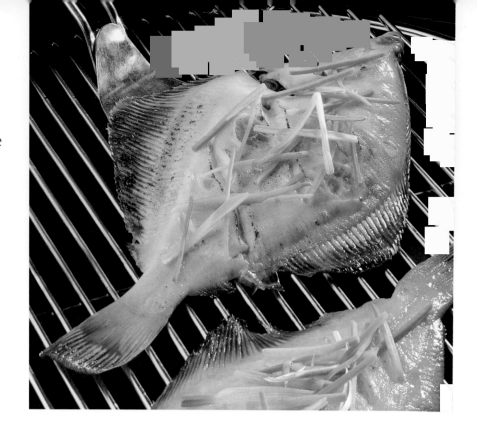

Japanese Flounder

SERVES 4

4 small flounders
6 tbsp soy sauce
2 tbsp sake or dry white wine
2 tbsp sesame oil
1 tbsp lemon juice
2 tbsp light brown sugar
1 tsp fresh gingerroot, grated
1 garlic clove, crushed

to garnish
1 small carrot
4 scallions

1 Wash the fish under cold running water and pat dry on paper towels.

2 Using a sharp knife, cut a few slashes into the sides of the fish so that they absorb the marinade.

3 Mix the soy sauce, sake or wine, sesame oil, lemon juice, sugar, ginger, and garlic together in a large, shallow dish.

4 Place the fish in the marinade and turn them until the fish are well coated on both sides. Cover and let marinate in the refrigerator for 1–6 hours.

5 Meanwhile, prepare the garnish. Cut the carrot into evenly sized thin sticks and shred the scallions.

6 Transfer the fish to a lit barbecue and cook over hot coals for 10 minutes, turning once.

7 Sprinkle the shredded scallions and carrot over the fish and transfer the fish to a serving dish. Serve immediately.

NUTRITION
Calories *207*; Sugars *9 g*; Protein *22 g*;
Carbohydrate *10 g*; Fat *8 g*; Saturates *1 g*

easy

1 hr 10 mins

10 mins

The cooking time may seem very long and indeed you could decrease it slightly if you prefer, but in Morocco they like their fish well cooked!

Hake Steaks *with* Chermoula

1 To make the marinade, mix the cilantro, parsley, garlic, cumin, coriander, paprika, cayenne, lemon juice, and olive oil together in a small bowl.

2 Wash the hake steaks under cold running water and pat dry with paper towels. Place the fish in an ovenproof dish and pour over the marinade. Cover with plastic wrap and let marinate in the refrigerator for at least 1 hour or preferably overnight.

3 Before cooking, sprinkle the olives over the fish. Cover the dish with foil.

4 Cook in a preheated oven, 325°F/160°C, for 35–40 minutes until the fish is tender. Transfer the fish to 4 large, warmed serving plates, garnish with lemon slices and serve with freshly cooked vegetables.

SERVES 4

4 hake steaks, about 8 oz/225 g each
½ cup pitted green olives
lemon slices, to garnish
freshly cooked vegetables, to serve

marinade
6 tbsp finely chopped cilantro
6 tbsp finely chopped fresh parsley
6 garlic cloves, crushed
1 tbsp ground cumin
1 tsp ground coriander
1 tbsp paprika
pinch of cayenne pepper
⅔ cup fresh lemon juice
1¼ cups olive oil

NUTRITION
Calories *590*; Sugars *1 g*; Protein *42 g*;
Carbohydrate *2 g*; Fat *46 g*; Saturates *7 g*

easy

1 hr 15 mins

35–40 mins

🍴 **COOK'S TIP**

For fried fish, remove the fish from the marinade and dust with seasoned flour. Cook in oil or clarified butter until golden. Warm through the marinade, but do not boil, and serve as a sauce with lemon slices.

This is a variation of a Middle Eastern recipe for stuffed mackerel, which involves removing the mackerel flesh, while leaving the skin intact, and then restuffing the skin. This version is much simpler.

Stuffed Mackerel

SERVES 4

4 large mackerel, cleaned
1 tbsp olive oil
1 small onion, sliced finely
1 tsp ground cinnamon
½ ground ginger
2 tbsp raisins
2 tbsp pine nuts, toasted
8 grape leaves in brine, drained
salt and pepper
lemon slices, to garnish

to garnish
mixed salad greens
plain boiled rice

1 Wash the fish under cold running water and pat dry with paper towels, then set aside. Heat the olive oil in a small skillet over low heat. Add the onion and cook gently for 5 minutes until softened. Add the cinnamon and ginger and cook for 30 seconds before adding the raisins and pine nuts. Remove from the heat and let cool.

2 Stuff each of the fish with one quarter of the stuffing mixture. Wrap each fish in 2 vine leaves, securing with toothpicks.

3 Transfer the fish to a lit barbecue or preheated ridged griddle and cook for about 5 minutes on each side until the vine leaves have scorched and the fish is tender. Transfer the fish to 4 large serving plates and serve with salad greens and plain boiled rice.

NUTRITION
Calories *488*; Sugars *12 g*; Protein *34 g*;
Carbohydrate *12 g*; Fat *34 g*; Saturates *6 g*

 easy

 10 mins

 20 mins

🧑‍🍳 **COOK'S TIP**

This stuffing works equally well with many other fish, including sea bass and red mullet.

These fishcakes make a
very satisfying and quick
midweek supper.

Tuna Fish Cakes

1 To make the tuna fish cakes, bring a large pan of lightly salted water to a boil
over medium heat. Add the potatoes and cook for 12–15 minutes until
tender. Drain well, then mash, leaving a few lumps, and set aside.

2 Heat the olive oil in a small skillet over low heat. Add the shallot and cook
for 5 minutes until softened. Add the garlic and thyme leaves and cook for
another 1 minute. Let cool slightly, then add to the potatoes with the tuna,
lemon rind, parsley, and salt and pepper to taste. Mix well, but leave texture.

3 Form the mixture into 6–8 cakes. Dip the cakes first in the flour, then the
egg and finally the bread crumbs to coat. Let chill for 30 minutes.

4 Meanwhile, make the tomato sauce. Place the olive oil, tomatoes, garlic,
sugar, lemon rind, basil, and salt and pepper to taste in a pan and bring to a
boil over low heat. Cover and let simmer for 30 minutes. Uncover and let
simmer for another 15 minutes until thickened.

5 Heat enough vegetable oil in a skillet to generously cover the bottom of the
skillet. When hot, add the fish cakes, in batches, and cook for 3–4 minutes on
each side until golden and crisp. Drain on paper towels while you cook the
remaining fish cakes. Serve hot with the tomato sauce.

SERVES 4

8 oz/225 g potatoes, peeled and cubed
1 tbsp olive oil
1 large shallot, chopped finely
1 garlic clove, chopped finely
1 tsp fresh thyme leaves
7 oz/200 g canned tuna in olive oil, drained
grated rind of ½ lemon
1 tbsp chopped fresh parsley
2–3 tbsp all-purpose flour
1 egg, beaten lightly
4 oz/115 g fresh bread crumbs
¼ cup vegetable oil, for pan-frying
salt and pepper

quick tomato sauce
2 tbsp olive oil
14 oz/400 g canned chopped tomatoes
1 garlic clove, crushed
½ tsp sugar
grated rind of ½ lemon
1 tbsp chopped fresh basil

NUTRITION
Calories *638*; Sugars *5 g*; Protein *35 g*;
Carbohydrate *38 g*; Fat *40 g*; Saturates *5 g*

  moderate

35 mins

1 hr 15 mins

This is called *Foo Yung* in China and is a classic dish, which may be flavored with any ingredients you have to hand.

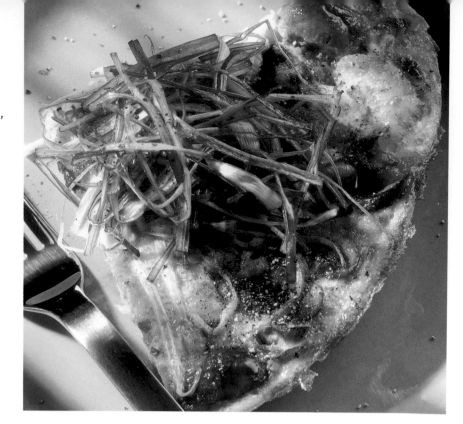

Shrimp Omelet

SERVES 4

3 tbsp corn oil
2 leeks, sliced
4 tbsp cornstarch
1 tsp salt
12 oz/350 g raw jumbo shrimp, peeled
6 oz/175 g mushrooms, sliced
6 oz/175 g bean sprouts
6 eggs
3 tbsp cold water
deep-fried leeks, to garnish (optional)

1 Heat the corn oil in a preheated wok or large, heavy-based skillet over medium heat. Add the leeks and stir-fry for 3 minutes.

2 Mix the cornstarch and salt together in a large bowl.

3 Add the shrimp to the cornstarch and salt mixture and toss to coat all over.

4 Add the shrimp to the wok or skillet and stir-fry for 2 minutes or until the shrimp have changed color and are almost cooked through.

5 Add the mushrooms and bean sprouts to the wok and stir-fry for another 2 minutes.

6 Beat the eggs with the water. Pour the egg mixture into the wok and cook until the egg sets, carefully turning the omelet over once. Turn the omelet out onto a clean cutting board, divide into 4 and serve hot, garnished with deep-fried leeks (if using).

NUTRITION
Calories 320; Sugars 1 g; Protein 31 g;
Carbohydrate 8 g; Fat 18 g; Saturates 4 g

moderate

10 mins

10 mins

 COOK'S TIP

If desired, divide the mixture for the filling into 4 at the end of Step 5, and make 4 individual omelets.

This is a very quick and tasty everyday supper dish. You could use a good-quality ready-made pesto to save even more time.

Sardines *with* Pesto

1 Wash the sardines under cold running water and pat dry on paper towels. Arrange on a broiler pan.

2 To make the pesto put the basil leaves, garlic, and pine nuts into a food processor and process until finely chopped. Transfer to a small bowl and stir in the Parmesan cheese and olive oil. Season to taste with salt and pepper.

3 Spread a little of the pesto over one side of the sardines and place under a preheated hot broiler for 3 minutes. Turn the fish, spread with more pesto, and broil for another 3 minutes until the sardines are cooked.

4 Transfer the fish to 4 serving plates, garnish with a few sprigs of fresh dill and lemon wedges. Serve immediately with extra pesto, garnished with strips of lemon rind.

SERVES 4

16 large sardines, scaled and gutted
2 loosely packed cups fresh basil leaves
2 garlic cloves, crushed
2 tbsp pine nuts, toasted
½ cup freshly grated Parmesan cheese
⅔ cup olive oil
salt and pepper

to serve
fresh dill sprigs
lemon wedges
strips of lemon rind

NUTRITION
Calories *617*; Sugars *0 g*; Protein *27 g*;
Carbohydrate *1 g*; Fat *56 g*; Saturates *11 g*

easy
25 mins
6 mins

🍳 COOK'S TIP

This treatment will also work well with other small oily fish such as herrings and pilchards.

A frittata is an Italian slow-cooked omelet, not dissimilar to the Spanish tortilla. Here it is filled with poached salmon, fresh herbs, and vegetables to make a substantial dish.

Salmon Frittata

SERVES 4

9 oz/250 g skinless, boneless salmon
3 fresh thyme sprigs
1 fresh parsley sprig, plus 2 tbsp chopped fresh parsley
5 black peppercorns
½ small onion, sliced
½ celery stalk, sliced
½ carrot, chopped
6 oz/175 g asparagus spears, chopped
3 oz/85 g baby carrots, halved
¼ cup butter
1 large onion, sliced finely
1 garlic clove, chopped finely
1 cup peas, fresh or frozen
8 eggs, beaten lightly
1 tbsp chopped fresh dill
salt and pepper

to serve
sour cream
salad greens
lemon wedges
crusty bread

NUTRITION
Calories *300*; Sugars *5 g*; Protein *22 g*;
Carbohydrate *7 g*; Fat *21 g*; Saturates *8 g*

         moderate

         15 mins

         1 hr

1 Place the salmon in a pan with a sprig of the thyme, the parsley sprig, peppercorns, onion, celery, and carrot. Cover the vegetables and fish with cold water and bring slowly to a boil over low heat. Remove the pan from the heat and let stand for 5 minutes. Lift the fish out of the the poaching liquid, flake the flesh and set aside. Discard the poaching liquid.

2 Bring a large pan of lightly salted water to a boil over medium heat. Add the asparagus and blanch for 2 minutes. Drain and refresh under cold running water. Blanch the carrots for 4 minutes. Drain and refresh under cold running water. Drain again and pat dry with paper towels. Set aside.

3 Heat half the butter in a large skillet over low heat. Add the onion and cook gently for 8–10 minutes until softened, but not colored. Add the garlic and remaining sprigs of thyme and cook for another 1 minute. Add the asparagus, carrots, and peas and heat through. Remove from the heat.

4 Add the vegetables to the eggs with the chopped parsley, dill, and salmon, and season to taste with salt and pepper. Stir briefly. Heat the remaining butter in the pan and return the mixture to the pan. Cover and cook over low heat for 10 minutes.

5 Transfer the frittata to a broiler pan and cook under a preheated medium–hot broiler for another 5 minutes until set and golden. Serve in wedges topped with sour cream, salad greens, lemon wedges, and fresh crusty bread.

You can use turbot and salmon instead of fillets for these brochettes. Remove the skin and bones yourself and chop the flesh into large chunks.

Mixed Seafood Brochettes

1 Chop the halibut and salmon into 8 pieces each. Thread on to 8 metal skewers, with the scallops and jumbo shrimp or langoustines, alternating with the bay leaves and lemon slices. Put into a non-metallic dish in a single layer, if possible.

2 Mix the olive oil, lemon rind, herbs, and pepper together and pour over the fish. Cover and let marinate for 2 hours, turning once or twice.

3 To make the lemon butter rice, bring a large pan of lightly salted water to a boil over medium heat. Add the rice and lemon rind, return to a boil and let simmer for 7–8 minutes until the rice is tender. Drain well and immediately stir in the lemon juice and butter. Season to taste with salt and pepper.

4 Meanwhile, lift the fish brochettes from their marinade and cook on a lit barbecue or under a preheated hot broiler for 8–10 minutes, turning regularly, until cooked through. Transfer to 4 large serving plates, garnish with lemon wedges and a few sprigs of fresh dill. Serve with the lemon butter rice.

SERVES 4

8 oz/225 g skinless, boneless halibut fillet
8 oz/225 g skinless, boneless salmon fillet
8 scallops
8 large jumbo shrimp or langoustines
16 bay leaves
1 lemon, sliced
4 tbsp olive oil
grated rind 1 lemon
4 tbsp chopped mixed herbs such as thyme, parsley, chives, and basil
salt and pepper

lemon butter rice

2 cups long-grain rice
grated rind and juice of 1 lemon
¼ cup butter

to garnish
lemon wedges
fresh dill sprigs

NUTRITION
Calories *455*; Sugars *0 g*; Protein *32 g*;
Carbohydrate *39 g*; Fat *20 g*; Saturates *9 g*

easy

2 hrs 15 mins

20 mins

 COOK'S TIP

If halibut is unavailable, then use another flat fish instead.

Marinated scallops and barbecued and served with couscous studded with colorful vegetables and fresh herbs.

Barbecued Scallops

SERVES 4

16 king scallops
3 tbsp olive oil
grated rind of 1 lime
2 tbsp chopped fresh basil
2 tbsp chopped fresh chives
1 garlic clove, chopped finely
pepper

bejeweled couscous

2 cups couscous
½ yellow bell pepper, seeded and halved
½ red bell pepper, seeded and halved
4 tbsp extra virgin olive oil
1 small cucumber, chopped into
    ½-inch/1-cm pieces
3 scallions, chopped finely
1 tbsp lime juice
2 tbsp shredded fresh basil
salt and pepper

to garnish

fresh basil leaves
lime wedges

NUTRITION

Calories *401*; Sugars *3 g*; Protein *20 g*;
Carbohydrate *34 g*; Fat *21 g*; Saturates *3 g*

moderate
2 hrs 15 mins
15 mins

1 Clean and trim the scallops as necessary. Put into a non-metallic dish. Mix the olive oil, lime rind, basil, chives, garlic, and pepper together in a bowl, then pour over the scallops. Cover and let marinate in the refrigerator for 2 hours.

2 Cook the couscous according to the package instructions, omitting any butter recommended. Brush the red and yellow bell pepper halves with a little of the olive oil and cook under a preheated hot broiler for 8–10 minutes, turning once, until the skins are charred and blistered and the flesh is tender. Put into a plastic bag and leave until cool enough to handle. When cool, peel off the skins and chop the flesh into ½-inch/1-cm pieces. Add to the couscous with the remaining olive oil, cucumber, scallions, lemon juice, and salt and pepper to taste. Set aside.

3 Lift the scallops from the marinade and thread onto 4 metal skewers. Transfer to a lit barbecue or preheated ridged griddle and cook for 1 minute on each side until charred and firm, but not quite cooked through. Remove from the heat and let rest for 2 minutes.

4 Stir the shredded basil into the couscous and transfer to 4 serving plates. Put a skewer on each, garnish with basil leaves and lime wedges and serve.

These crisp little vegetable and shrimp cakes make an ideal light lunch or supper, accompanied with a salad.

Shrimp Rostis

1 To make the salsa, mix the tomatoes, mango, chile, red onion, cilantro, chives, olive oil, lemon juice, and seasoning together in a bowl. Let stand to let the flavors infuse.

2 Using a food processor or the fine blade of a box grater, finely grate the potatoes, celeriac, carrot, and onion. Mix together with the shrimp, flour, and egg. Season well with salt and pepper and set aside.

3 Divide the shrimp mixture into 8 equal portions and press each into a lightly greased 4-inch/10-cm cutter (if you only have 1 cutter, then simply shape the rostis individually).

4 Heat a shallow layer of vegetable oil in a large skillet over medium heat. When hot, transfer the vegetable and prawn cakes, still in the cutters, to the skillet, in batches if necessary. When the oil sizzles underneath, remove the cutter. Cook gently, pressing down with a spatula, for 6–8 minutes on each side, until crisp and browned and the vegetables are tender. Drain on paper towels. Serve immediately, while still hot, with the tomato salsa and mixed salad greens.

 COOK'S TIP

The shrimps can be replaced with small flakes of cod, salmon, or tuna.

SERVES 4

12 oz/350 g potatoes, peeled
12 oz/350 g celeriac
1 carrot
½ small onion
8 oz/225 g cooked peeled shrimp, thawed if frozen and well-drained on paper towels
¼ cup all-purpose flour
1 egg, beaten lightly
¼ cup vegetable oil, for pan-frying
salt and pepper
mixed salad greens, to serve

cherry tomato salsa

8 oz/225 g mixed cherry tomatoes such as baby plum, yellow, orange, pear, cut into fourths
½ small mango, diced finely
1 fresh red chile, seeded and finely chopped
½ small red onion, chopped finely
1 tbsp chopped fresh cilantro
1 tbsp chopped fresh chives
2 tbsp olive oil
2 tsp lemon juice

NUTRITION

Calories *445*; Sugars *9 g*; Protein *19 g*; Carbohydrate *29 g*; Fat *29 g*; Saturates *4 g*

 moderate

20 mins

12–16 mins

This dish is much revered in both Belgium and France. Try the chips with a little homemade mayonnaise (see Fish and Chips page 96) and enjoy a truly Belgian feast.

Moules Marinières

SERVES 4

2 lb/900 g live mussels
2 shallots, chopped finely
2 garlic cloves, chopped finely
²⁄₃ cup dry white wine
2 tbsp chopped fresh parsley
salt and pepper

chips
2 lb/900 g potatoes, peeled
2 cups vegetable oil, for deep-frying
salt

to serve (optional)
lemon wedges
Mayonnaise (see page 96)

NUTRITION
Calories 88; Sugars 1 g; Protein 9 g;
Carbohydrate 4 g; Fat 1 g; Saturates 0.5 g

easy

15 mins

30 mins

1 Clean the mussels by scrubbing or scraping the shells and pulling out any beards that are attached to them. Discard any mussels with broken shells or any that refuse to close when tapped.

2 To make the chips, cut the potatoes into thin strips, about ½ inch/1 cm thick. Fill a large saucepan or chip pan about one-third full with vegetable oil and heat to 275°F/140°C, or until a cube of bread browns in 1 minute. Add the chips in 3 batches and cook for 5–6 minutes until the chips are tender, but not browned. Drain on paper towels.

3 Put the mussels into a large pan with the shallots, garlic, and white wine. Cook, covered, over high heat for 3–4 minutes until all the mussels have opened. Discard any mussels that remain closed. Add the parsley and season to taste with salt and pepper. Keep warm.

4 Increase the temperature of the oil to 375°F/190°C, or until a cube of bread browns in 30 seconds. Cook the chips, again in 3 batches, for 2–3 minutes until golden and crisp. Drain on paper towels and sprinkle with salt.

5 Divide the mussels among 4 large serving bowls. Divide the chips among smaller bowls or plates and serve with lemon wedges and plenty of mayonnaise for dipping chips, if desired.

This recipe conjures up southern France—tomatoes, wine, herbs, and garlic combine to make a flavorful mussel stew.

Provençal Mussels

1 Clean the mussels by scrubbing or scraping the shells and pulling out any beards that are attached to them. Discard any mussels with broken shells or that refuse to close when tapped. Put the mussels in a large pan with just the water that clings to their shells. Cook, covered, over high heat for 3–4 minutes until all the mussels have opened. Discard any mussels that remain closed. Strain, reserving the cooking liquid. Set aside.

2 Heat the olive oil in a large pan over low heat. Add the onion and cook gently for 8–10 minutes until softened, but not colored. Add the garlic and thyme and cook for another 1 minute. Add the red wine and let simmer rapidly until reduced and syrupy. Add the tomatoes and strained, reserved mussel cooking liquid and bring to a boil. Cover and let simmer for 30 minutes. Uncover and cook for 15 minutes.

3 Add the mussels and cook for another 5 minutes until heated through. Stir in the parsley, season to taste with salt and pepper and serve.

SERVES 4

2 lb/900 g live mussels
3 tbsp olive oil
1 onion, chopped finely
3 garlic cloves, chopped finely
2 tsp fresh thyme leaves
⅔ cup red wine
14 oz/400 g canned chopped tomatoes
2 tbsp chopped fresh parsley
salt and pepper

  COOK'S TIP

Replace the mussels with an equal quantity of clams if you prefer.

NUTRITION
Calories *194*; Sugars *5 g*; Protein *12 g*;
Carbohydrate *9 g*; Fat *10 g*; Saturates *2 g*

★★★   moderate

🌐   10 mins

🕐   1 hr

This is based on a Sicilian dish combining broccoli and anchovies, but in this recipe lemon and garlic have been added for more flavor.

Tagliatelle *with* Broccoli *and* Anchovies

SERVES 4

6 tbsp olive oil
½ cup fresh white bread crumbs
1 lb/450 g broccoli, cut into small florets
12 oz/350 g dried tagliatelle
4 canned anchovy fillets, drained
   and chopped
2 garlic cloves, sliced
grated rind of 1 lemon
large pinch of chili flakes
salt and pepper
freshly grated Parmesan cheese, to serve

1 Heat 2 tablespoons of the olive oil in a skillet over medium heat. Add the bread crumbs and stir-fry for 4–5 minutes until golden and crisp. Drain on paper towels.

2 Bring a large pan of lightly salted water to a boil over medium heat. Add the broccoli and blanch for 3 minutes, then drain and set aside the water. Refresh the broccoli under cold running water and drain again. Pat dry on paper towels and set aside. Bring the water back to a boil and add the tagliatelle. Cook according to the package directions until tender, but still firm to the bite.

3 Meanwhile, heat another 2 tablespoons of the oil in a skillet over medium heat. Add the anchovies and cook for 1 minute, then mash with a wooden spoon to a paste. Add the garlic, lemon rind, and chili flakes and cook gently for 2 minutes. Add the broccoli and cook for another 3–4 minutes until hot.

4 Drain the pasta and add to the broccoli with the remaining 2 tablespoons of olive oil. Season to taste with salt and pepper. Toss together. Divide the tagliatelle among 4 large serving plates and top with the fried bread crumbs and Parmesan cheese. Serve immediately.

NUTRITION
Calories 529; Sugars 4 g; Protein 17 g;
Carbohydrate 75 g; Fat 20 g; Saturates 3 g

easy

10 mins

30 mins

The story goes that this was a dish made and eaten by Italian women who needed a quick and simple meal to keep them going. Most of the ingredients you will have in the pantry.

Pasta Puttanesca

1 Heat the olive oil in a pan over low heat. Add the onion, anchovies, and chili flakes and cook for 10 minutes until softened and starting to brown. Add the garlic and cook for 30 seconds.

2 Add the tomatoes and tomato paste and bring to a boil. Let simmer gently for 10 minutes.

3 Meanwhile, bring a large pan of water to a boil over medium heat. Add the spaghetti and cook according to the package directions until tender, but still firm to the bite.

4 Add the olives, capers, and sun-dried tomatoes to the sauce. Let simmer for another 2–3 minutes. Season to taste with salt and pepper.

5 Drain the pasta well and stir in the sauce. Toss well. Transfer to 4 large serving plates, garnish with mixed fresh herbs and serve immediately.

SERVES 4

3 tbsp extra virgin olive oil
1 large red onion, chopped finely
4 canned anchovy fillets, drained
pinch of chile flakes
2 garlic cloves, chopped finely
14 oz/400 g canned chopped tomatoes
2 tbsp tomato paste
8 oz/225 g dried spaghetti
½ cup pitted black olives, chopped coarsely
½ cup pitted green olives, chopped coarsely
1 tbsp capers, drained and rinsed
4 sun-dried tomatoes, chopped coarsely
salt and pepper

to garnish
mixed fresh herbs
fresh tomato wedges

NUTRITION
Calories *359*; Sugars *10 g*; Protein *10 g*;
Carbohydrate *51 g*; Fat *14 g*; Saturates *2 g*

easy

5 mins

25 mins

🍲 COOK'S TIP

Chili flakes are available from large supermarkets, but if you cannot find them, then use 1 fresh red chile, seeded and sliced instead.

A rich dish of layers of pasta, with seafood and mushrooms in a tomato sauce, topped with béchamel sauce and baked until golden.

Seafood Lasagne

SERVES 4

¼ cup butter
6 tbsp all-purpose flour
1 tsp mustard powder
2½ cups milk
2 tbsp olive oil, plus extra for oiling
1 onion, chopped
2 garlic cloves, chopped finely
1 tbsp fresh thyme leaves
3 cups mixed mushrooms, sliced
⅔ cup white wine
14 oz/400 g canned chopped tomatoes
1 lb/450 g mixed skinless white fish
    fillets, cubed
8 oz/225 g fresh scallops, trimmed
4–6 sheets fresh lasagne
8 oz/225 g mozzarella cheese, chopped
salt and pepper

NUTRITION
Calories 790; Sugars 23 g; Protein 55 g;
Carbohydrate 74 g; Fat 32 g; Saturates 19 g

   moderate
    30 mins
    1 hr 20 mins

1 Melt the butter in a pan over low heat. Add the flour and mustard powder and stir until smooth. Let simmer gently for 2 minutes without coloring. Gradually add the milk, whisking until smooth. Bring to a boil and let simmer for 2 minutes. Remove the pan from the heat and set aside. Cover the surface of the sauce with plastic wrap to prevent a skin forming.

2 Heat the olive oil in a skillet over low heat. Add the onion, garlic, and thyme and cook gently for 5 minutes until softened. Add the mushrooms and cook for another 5 minutes until softened. Stir in the wine and boil rapidly until nearly evaporated. Stir in the tomatoes. Bring to a boil and let simmer, covered, for 15 minutes. Season to taste with salt and pepper and set aside.

3 Lightly oil a lasagne dish with a little olive oil. Spoon half the tomato sauce over the bottom of the dish and top with half the fish and scallops.

4 Layer half the lasagne over the fish, pour over half the white sauce, add half the mozzarella cheese. Repeat these layers, finishing with the white sauce and mozzarella cheese.

5 Bake in a preheated oven, 400°F/200°C, for 35–40 minutes until bubbling and golden and the fish is cooked through. Remove from the oven and let stand on a heat resistant surface for 10 minutes before serving.

This is a very full-flavored and elegant-looking dish, especially if you can find small clams, which often have richly colored shells.

Spaghetti *al* Vongole

1 Put the clams into a pan with just the water that clings to their shells and cook, covered, over high heat for 3–4 minutes, shaking the pan occasionally, until all the clams have opened. Remove from the heat and strain. Set aside the cooking liquid. Discard any clams that remain closed. Set aside.

2 Heat the olive oil in a pan over low heat. Add the onion and cook for about 10 minutes until softened, but not colored. Add the garlic and thyme and cook for another 30 seconds. Increase the heat and add the wine. Let simmer rapidly until reduced and syrupy. Add the tomatoes and the reserved clam cooking liquid. Cover and let simmer for 15 minutes. Uncover and let simmer for another 15 minutes until thickened. Season to taste with salt and pepper.

3 Meanwhile, bring a large pan of lightly salted water to a boil over medium heat. Add the spaghetti and cook according to the package directions until tender, but still firm to the bite. Drain well and return to the pan.

4 Add the clams to the tomato sauce and heat through for 2–3 minutes. Add the parsley and stir. Add the tomato sauce to the pasta and toss together until the pasta is coated in the sauce. Transfer to a serving dish and garnish with thyme. Serve at once.

SERVES 4

2 lb/900 g live clams, scrubbed
2 tbsp olive oil
1 large onion, chopped finely
2 garlic cloves, chopped finely
1 tsp fresh thyme leaves
²⁄₃ cup white wine
14 oz/400 g canned chopped tomatoes
12 oz/350 g dried spaghetti
1 tbsp chopped fresh parsley
salt and pepper
fresh thyme leaves, to garnish

NUTRITION

Calories 471; Sugars 9 g; Protein 24 g; Carbohydrate 75 g; Fat 8 g; Saturates 1 g

easy

10 mins

1 hr

🍽 **COOK'S TIP**

If you are only able to get very large clams, set aside a few in their shells to garnish and shell the rest.

This is a very quick dish that is ideal for midweek meals as it is so simple to prepare, but full of flavor.

Linguine *with* Sardines

SERVES 4

8 sardines, filleted
1 fennel bulb
4 tbsp olive oil
3 garlic cloves, sliced
1 tsp chile flakes
12 oz/350 g dried linguine
½ tsp finely grated lemon rind
1 tbsp lemon juice
2 tbsp pine nuts, toasted
2 tbsp chopped fresh parsley, plus
    extra for sprinkling
salt and pepper
fresh herbs, to garnish

NUTRITION
Calories 547; Sugars 5 g; Protein 23 g;
Carbohydrate 68 g; Fat 23 g; Saturates 3 g

easy

10 mins

12 mins

1 Wash the sardine fillets under cold running water and pat dry with paper towels. Coarsely chop into large pieces and set aside. Trim the fennel bulb and slice very thinly.

2 Heat 2 tablespoons of the olive oil in a large skillet over medium heat. Add the garlic and chile flakes and cook for 1 minute, then add the fennel. Cook over a medium–high heat for 4–5 minutes until softened. Add the sardine pieces and cook for another 3–4 minutes until just cooked.

3 Meanwhile, bring a large pan of lightly salted water to a boil over medium heat. Add the linguine and cook according to the package directions until tender, but still firm to the bite. Drain well and return to the pan.

4 Add the lemon rind, lemon juice, pine nuts, parsley, and seasoning to the sardines and toss together. Add to the pasta with the remaining olive oil and toss together gently. Transfer the pasta to 4 large serving bowls, sprinkle with parsley and garnish with fresh herbs. Serve immediately.

COOK'S TIP

Set aside 2 tablespoons of the pasta cooking water and add to the pasta with the sauce if the mixture seems a little dry.

Although it is quite time consuming to make and fill your own pasta, the flavor and texture are unbeatable.

Crab Ravioli

1 To make the bell pepper sauce, brush the pepper pieces with the olive oil. Place under a preheated hot broiler for 3–4 minutes on each side until the skin is charred and blistered and the flesh is tender. Remove from the heat and place in a plastic bag until cool enough to handle. Peel off the skin and discard. Put the flesh into a food processor or blender, add the butter, lime juice and seasoning and process until smooth. Set aside.

2 To make the pasta, strain the flour and salt into a bowl. Make a well in the center and add the eggs, egg yolk, oil, and enough water to make a firm dough. Knead for 5 minutes. Wrap in plastic wrap and let chill.

3 Meanwhile, mix the shrimp, crab, chervil, chives, parsley, lime rind, cream, and salt and pepper together in a bowl and set aside.

4 Divide the pasta dough into 8 pieces. Using a pasta machine, roll out each piece as thinly as possible. Dust the surface with flour and top with 1 sheet of pasta. Place 1 teaspoon of filling at 1-inch/2.5-cm intervals along the dough. Brush around the filling with water, then place a second sheet of pasta on top.

5 Press down firmly around each mound of filling, then cut out the ravioli and place on a well-floured dishtowel. Repeat with the other pasta and filling.

6 Bring a large pan of lightly salted water to a boil over medium heat. Add the ravioli and boil for 3–4 minutes until tender, but still firm to the bite. Drain well and toss with the bell pepper sauce. Transfer to 4 large serving plates, garnish with lime wedges, chives, and parsley. Serve immediately.

SERVES 4

2 cups all-purpose flour, plus extra for dusting
1 tsp salt
2 eggs, plus 1 egg yolk
1 tbsp olive oil
8 oz/225 g raw shrimp, chopped finely
8 oz/225 g white crabmeat
1 tbsp chopped fresh chervil
1 tbsp chopped fresh chives
1 tbsp chopped fresh parsley
1 tsp grated rind lime
4 tbsp heavy cream
salt and pepper

red bell pepper sauce
½ large red bell pepper, seeded and halved
1 tsp olive oil, for brushing
¼ cup unsalted butter, softened
1 tbsp lime juice

to garnish
lime wedges
chopped fresh chives
fresh parsley sprigs

NUTRITION
Calories *610*; Sugars *3 g*; Protein *33 g*;
Carbohydrate *45 g*; Fat *34 g*; Saturates *18 g*

  moderate

30 mins

10 mins

This dish is extremely easy, yet the flavor is as impressive as a recipe over which you have slaved for hours.

Spaghettini *with* Crab

SERVES 4

1 dressed crab, about 1 lb/450 g including the shell
12 oz/350 g dried spaghettini
6 tbsp best quality extra virgin olive oil
1 fresh red chile, seeded and finely chopped
2 garlic cloves, chopped finely
3 tbsp chopped fresh parsley
1 tsp finely grated lemon rind
2 tbsp lemon juice
salt and pepper
lemon wedges, to garnish

1 Scoop the meat from the crab shell into a bowl. Mix the white and brown meat lightly together and set aside.

2 Bring a large pan of lightly salted water to a boil over medium heat. Add the spaghettini and cook according to the package directions until tender, but still firm to the bite. Drain well and return to the pan.

3 Meanwhile, heat 2 tablespoons of the olive oil in a skillet over low heat. When hot, add the chile and garlic. Cook for 30 seconds before adding the crabmeat, parsley, lemon juice, and lemon rind. Stir-fry for another 1 minute until the crab is just heated through.

4 Add the crab mixture to the pasta with the remaining olive oil and salt and pepper to taste. Toss together thoroughly and transfer to 4 large serving plates. Garnish with lemon wedges and serve immediately.

NUTRITION
Calories *488*; Sugars *3 g*; Protein *13 g*;
Carbohydrate *65 g*; Fat *19 g*; Saturates *3 g*

  easy

  10 mins

10 mins

🍳 **COOK'S TIP**

If you prefer to buy your own fresh crab you will need a large crab weighing about 2 lb 4 oz/1 kg.

The classic Italian combination of pasta and tuna is enhanced in this recipe with a delicious parsley sauce.

Spaghetti *al* Tonno

1 Drain the tuna. Put the tuna into a food processor or blender, along with with the anchovies, 1 cup of the olive oil and the Italian parsley and process until the sauce is very smooth.

2 Spoon the crème fraîche into the food processor or blender and process for a few seconds to blend thoroughly. Season to taste with salt and pepper.

3 Bring a large pan of lightly salted water to a boil over medium heat. Add the spaghetti and cook according to the package directions until tender, but still firm to the bite.

4 Drain the spaghetti, return to the pan and place over medium heat. Add the butter and toss well to coat. Spoon in the sauce and quickly toss into the spaghetti, using 2 forks.

5 Remove the pan from the heat and transfer the spaghetti to 4 warmed serving plates. Garnish with the olives and a few sprigs of fresh parsley and serve immediately.

SERVES 4

7 oz/200 g canned tuna
2 oz/55 g canned anchovy fillets, drained
1 cup olive oil
1 cup coarsely chopped flatleaf parsley
²/₃ cup crème fraîche or mascarpone cheese
1 lb/450 g dried spaghetti
2 tbsp butter
salt and pepper

to garnish
pitted black olives
fresh flatleaf parsley sprigs

NUTRITION
Calories 1065; Sugars 3 g; Protein 27 g;
Carbohydrate 52 g; Fat 85 g; Saturates 18 g

  easy

 10 mins

15 mins

FISH & SEAFOOD

Fideua is a pasta dish from the area south of Valencia, in western Spain. It is very like a paella, but is made with very fine pasta instead of rice.

Fideua

SERVES 6

3 tbsp olive oil
1 large onion, chopped
2 garlic cloves, chopped finely
pinch of saffron strands, crushed
½ tsp paprika
3 tomatoes, peeled, seeded, and chopped
12 oz/350 g egg vermicelli, broken coarsely into 2-inch/5-cm lengths
⅔ cup white wine
1¼ cups fish bouillon
12 large raw jumbo shrimp
18 live mussels, scrubbed and bearded
12 oz/350 g cleaned squid, cut into rings
18 large live clams, scrubbed
2 tbsp chopped fresh parsley
salt and pepper

1 Heat the olive oil in a large skillet or paella pan over low heat. Add the onion and cook gently for 5 minutes until softened. Add the garlic and cook for another 30 seconds. Add the saffron and paprika and stir well. Add the tomatoes and cook for another 2–3 minutes until they have collapsed.

2 Add the vermicelli and stir well. Add the white wine and boil rapidly until the wine has been absorbed.

3 Add the fish bouillon, shrimp, mussels, squid, and clams. Stir and let simmer for 10 minutes until the shrimp and squid are cooked through and the mussels and clams have opened. The bouillon should be almost absorbed.

4 Add the parsley and season to taste with salt and pepper. Transfer to 6 large, warmed serving bowls and serve immediately.

NUTRITION
Calories 373; Sugars 4 g; Protein 23 g;
Carbohydrate 52 g; Fat 8 g; Saturates 1 g

 moderate

 40 mins

40 mins

20 mins

 COOK'S TIP

Use whatever combination of seafood you prefer. Try langoustines, shrimp, clams, and monkfish.

The classic Thai noodle dish is flavored with fish sauce, roasted peanuts, and shrimp.

Thai Noodles

1 Drain the shrimp on paper towels to remove excess moisture. Set aside. Cook the rice noodles according to the package directions. Drain well and set aside.

2 Heat the vegetable oil in a preheated wok or large skillet over high heat. Add the garlic and stir-fry until just golden. Add the egg and stir quickly to break it up. Cook for a few seconds.

3 Add the shrimp and noodles, scraping down the sides of the wok to ensure they mix with the egg and garlic.

4 Add the lemon juice, Thai fish sauce, sugar, half the peanuts, cayenne pepper, the scallions, and half the bean sprouts, stirring quickly all the time. Cook over a high heat for another 2 minutes until heated through.

5 Transfer to 4 large serving plates, top with the remaining peanuts and bean sprouts and sprinkle with the fresh cilantro. Garnish with lemon wedges and serve.

SERVES 4

12 oz/350 g cooked peeled jumbo shrimp
4 oz/115 g flat rice noodles or rice vermicelli
4 tbsp vegetable oil
2 garlic cloves, chopped finely
1 egg
2 tbsp lemon juice
1½ tbsp Thai fish sauce
½ tsp sugar
2 tbsp chopped, roasted peanuts
½ tsp cayenne pepper
2 scallions, cut into 1-inch/2.5-cm pieces
1¾ oz/50 g fresh bean sprouts
1 tbsp chopped fresh cilantro
lemon wedges, to garnish

NUTRITION
Calories *344*; Sugars *2 g*; Protein *21 g*; Carbohydrate *27 g*; Fat *17 g*; Saturates *2 g*

easy

10 mins

5 mins

🍲 COOK'S TIP

This is a basic dish to which lots of different cooked seafood could be added. Cooked squid rings, mussels, and langoustines would all work well.

Originally, kedgeree or khichri was a Hindi dish of rice and lentils, varied with fish or meat in all kinds of ways. It has come to be a dish of rice, spices, and smoked fish served with hard-cooked eggs, often for breakfast.

Kedgeree

SERVES 4

1 lb/450 g undyed smoked haddock fillet
2 tbsp olive oil
1 large onion, chopped
2 garlic cloves, chopped finely
½ tsp ground turmeric
½ tsp ground cumin
1 tsp ground coriander
¾ cup basmati rice
4 medium eggs
2 tbsp butter
1 tbsp chopped fresh parsley

NUTRITION
Calories *457*; Sugars *3 g*; Protein *33 g*;
Carbohydrate *40 g*; Fat *18 g*; Saturates *6 g*

easy

15 mins

35 mins

1 Put the haddock fillet in a large, shallow dish and pour over enough boiling water to cover. Let stand for 10 minutes. Lift the fish from the cooking water, discard the skin and bones, and, using a fork, flake the fish. Set aside both the fish and the cooking water.

2 Heat the olive oil in a large pan over medium heat. Add the onion and cook for 10 minutes until starting to brown. Add the garlic and cook for another 30 seconds. Add the turmeric, cumin, and coriander and cook for 30 seconds until the spices smell fragrant. Add the rice and stir well.

3 Measure 1½ cups of the haddock cooking water and add to the pan. Stir well and bring to a boil. Cover and cook over very low heat for 12–15 minutes until the rice is tender and the bouillon is absorbed.

4 Meanwhile, bring a small pan of water to a boil over medium heat. Add the eggs, return to a boil and cook for 8 minutes. Immediately drain the eggs and refresh under cold running water to stop them cooking. Set aside.

5 Add the reserved fish pieces, the butter, and parsley to the rice. Turn onto a large serving dish. Shell and cut the eggs into fourths and arrange on top of the rice. Serve immediately.

This is a modern version of the classic dish, using smoked salmon as well as fresh salmon, and lots of herbs. This is suitable for a smart dinner party and would serve six as an appetizer or four as a main course.

Modern Kedgeree

1 Melt the butter with the olive oil in a large pan over low heat. Add the onion and cook gently for 10 minutes until softened, but not colored. Add the garlic and cook for another 30 seconds.

2 Add the rice and cook for 2–3 minutes, stirring constantly, until transparent. Add the fish bouillon and stir well. Bring to a boil, cover and let simmer very gently for 10 minutes.

3 Remove the pan form the heat and add the salmon fillet and the smoked salmon. Stir well, adding a little more bouillon or water if it seems dry. Return to the heat and cook for another 6–8 minutes until the fish and rice are tender and all the bouillon has been absorbed.

4 Remove from the heat and stir in the cream, dill, and scallions. Season to taste with salt and pepper and transfer to a large serving dish. Garnish with lemon slices and a few sprigs of fresh dill. Serve immediately.

SERVES 4

2 tbsp butter
1 tbsp olive oil
1 onion, chopped finely
1 garlic clove, chopped finely
¾ cup long-grain rice
1⅔ cups fish bouillon
6 oz/175 g skinless, boneless salmon fillet, chopped
3 oz/85 g smoked salmon, chopped
2 tbsp heavy cream
2 tbsp chopped fresh dill
3 scallions, chopped finely
salt and pepper

to garnish
lemon slices
fresh dill sprigs

COOK'S TIP

Use smoked salmon trimmings for a budget dish.

NUTRITION
Calories 370; Sugars 3 g; Protein 10 g; Carbohydrate 39 g; Fat 19 g; Saturates 9 g

 easy

10 mins

35 mins

Jambalaya is a dish of Cajun origin. There are as many versions of this dish as there are people who cook it. Here is a straightforward one, using shrimp, chicken, and smoked sausage.

Jambalaya

SERVES 4

2 tbsp vegetable oil
2 onions, chopped coarsely
1 green bell pepper, seeded and
    coarsely chopped
2 celery sticks, chopped coarsely
3 garlic cloves, chopped finely
2 tsp paprika
10½ oz/300 g skinless, boneless chicken
    breasts, chopped
3½ oz/100 g boudin sausages, chopped
3 tomatoes, peeled and chopped
2 cups long-grain rice
3¾ cups hot chicken or fish bouillon
1 tsp dried oregano
2 bay leaves
12 large jumbo shrimp tails
4 scallions, chopped finely
2 tbsp chopped fresh parsley
salt and pepper
fresh herbs, to garnish

NUTRITION

Calories 283; Sugars 3 g; Protein 33 g;
Carbohydrate 40 g; Fat 18 g; Saturates 6 g

easy

45 mins

35 mins

1 Heat the vegetable oil in a large skillet over low heat. Add the onions, bell pepper, celery, and garlic and cook for 8–10 minutes until all the vegetables have softened. Add the paprika and cook for another 30 seconds. Add the chicken and sausages and cook for 8–10 minutes until lightly browned. Add the tomatoes and cook for 2–3 minutes until they have collapsed.

2 Add the rice to the pan and stir well. Pour in the hot bouillon, oregano, and bay leaves and stir well. Cover and let simmer for 10 minutes.

3 Add the shrimp and stir well. Cover again and cook for another 6–8 minutes until the rice is tender and the shrimp are cooked through.

4 Stir in the scallions and parsley, and season to taste with salt and pepper. Transfer to a large serving dish, garnish with fresh herbs and serve.

🍳 COOK'S TIP

Jambalaya is a dish with many variations—use whatever you have on hand. Boudin is a classic Cajun sausage. Any spicy sausage would also work.

This is a special occasion dish, just for two. You could easily double the recipe for a dinner party.

Lobster Risotto

1 To prepare the lobster, remove the claws by twisting. Crack the claws using the back of a large knife and set aside. Split the body lengthwise. Remove and discard the intestinal vein, which runs down the tail, the stomach sack, and the spongy looking gills. Remove the meat from the tail and coarsely chop. Set aside with the claws.

2 Heat half the butter and the olive oil in a large skillet over low heat. Add the onion and cook for 4–5 minutes until softened. Add the garlic and cook for another 30 seconds. Add the thyme and rice. Stir well for 1–2 minutes, until the rice is well coated in the butter and oil and starts to look translucent.

3 Keep the bouillon on low heat. Increase the heat under the skillet to medium and start adding the bouillon, a ladleful at a time, stirring well between additions. Continue until all the bouillon has been absorbed. This should take 20–25 minutes.

4 Add the lobster meat and claws. Stir in the wine, increasing the heat. When the wine is absorbed, remove from the heat and stir in the peppercorns, remaining butter, and parsley. Let stand for 1 minute. Transfer to 2 serving plates. Garnish with lemon slices and a few sprigs of fresh dill to serve.

SERVES 2

1 cooked lobster, about 14 oz–1 lb/
   400 g–450 g
¼ cup butter
1 tbsp olive oil
1 onion, chopped finely
1 garlic clove, chopped finely
1 tsp fresh thyme leaves
¾ cup arborio rice
2½ cups hot fish bouillon
⅔ cup sparkling wine
1 tsp green or pink peppercorns in brine,
   drained and coarsely chopped
1 tbsp chopped fresh parsley

to garnish
lemon slices
fresh dill sprigs

NUTRITION
Calories *487*; Sugars *8 g*; Protein *10 g*;
Carbohydrate *86 g*; Fat *10 g*; Saturates *2 g*

  moderate

45 mins

35 mins

COOK'S TIP

For a slightly cheaper version substitute 1 lb/450 g shrimp for the lobster.

This unusual and striking dish with fresh shrimp and asparagus is very simple to prepare and ideal for impromptu dinner parties.

Shrimp *and* Asparagus Risotto

SERVES 4

5 cups vegetable bouillon
12 oz/350 g asparagus, cut into
    2-inch/5-cm lengths
2 tbsp olive oil
1 onion, chopped finely
1 garlic clove, chopped finely
1½ cups arborio rice
1 lb/450 g raw jumbo shrimp,
    peeled and deveined
2 tbsp olive paste or tapenade
2 tbsp chopped fresh basil
salt and pepper

to garnish
fresh Parmesan cheese shavings
cooked whole shrimp
fresh dill sprigs

1 Bring the bouillon to a boil in a pan over low heat. Add the asparagus and cook for 3 minutes until just tender. Strain, and set aside the bouillon, and refresh the asparagus under cold running water. Drain and set aside.

2 Heat the olive oil in a large skillet over low heat. Add the onion and cook for 5 minutes until softened. Add the garlic and cook for 30 seconds. Add the rice and stir for 1–2 minutes until coated with the oil and slightly translucent.

3 Keep the bouillon on low heat. Increase the heat under the skillet to medium and start adding the bouillon, a ladleful at a time, stirring well between additions. Continue until almost all the bouillon has been absorbed. This should take 20–25 minutes.

4 Add the shrimp and asparagus with the last ladleful of bouillon and cook for another 5 minutes until the shrimp and rice are tender and the bouillon has been absorbed. Remove from the heat.

5 Stir in the olive paste, basil, and salt and pepper and let stand for 1 minute. Transfer to 4 serving bowls and garnish with Parmesan cheese shavings, whole shrimp, and a few sprigs of fresh parsley. Serve immediately.

NUTRITION
Calories *566*; Sugars *4 g*; Protein *30 g*;
Carbohydrate *86 g*; Fat *14 g*; Saturates *2 g*

       moderate

🕐   55 mins

🕐   40 mins

A Thai-influenced dish of rice, cooked in coconut milk, with spicy cooked monkfish, and fresh peas.

Spicy Coconut Rice *with* Monkfish

1 Put both chile, chili flakes, garlic, saffron, mint, olive oil, and lemon juice into a food processor or blender and process until finely chopped, but not smooth.

2 Put the monkfish into a non-metallic dish and pour over the spice paste, mixing well. Cover and let marinate in the refrigerator for 20 minutes.

3 Heat a large pan over medium heat until very hot. Using a draining spoon, lift the monkfish from the marinade and add in batches to the hot pan. Cook for 3–4 minutes until browned and firm. Remove with a draining spoon and set aside.

4 Add the onion and remaining marinade to the same pan and cook for about 5 minutes until softened and lightly browned. Add the rice and stir until well coated. Add the tomatoes and coconut milk. Bring to a boil, cover and let simmer very gently for 15 minutes. Stir in the peas, season to taste with salt and pepper and arrange the fish over the top. Cover with foil and continue to cook over very low heat for 5 minutes. Transfer to 4 large serving plates and garnish with lemon slices and chopped cilantro. Serve.

SERVES 4

1 fresh red chile, seeded and chopped
1 tsp chili flakes
2 garlic cloves, chopped
2 pinches of saffron threads
3 tbsp coarsely chopped mint leaves
4 tbsp olive oil
2 tbsp lemon juice
12 oz/350 g monkfish fillet, cut into
    bite-size pieces
1 onion, chopped finely
2 cups long-grain rice
14 oz/400 g canned chopped tomatoes
3/4 cup coconut milk
3/4 cup peas
salt and pepper

to garnish
lemon slices
2 tbsp chopped fresh cilantro

NUTRITION
Calories *440*; Sugars *8 g*; Protein *22 g*;
Carbohydrate *60 g*; Fat *14 g*; Saturates *2 g*

 easy

30 mins

 30 mins

COOK'S TIP

When marinating fish, make sure the fish is placed in a large, shallow, non-metallic dish and covered with plastic wrap.

Based on a traditional Cuban recipe, this dish is similar to Spanish paella, but it has the added kick of dark rum. A meal in one, it needs only a simple salad accompaniment, if desired.

Fish *and* Rice *with* Dark Rum

SERVES 4

1 lb/450 g firm white fish fillets, such as cod or monkfish, skinned and cut into 1-inch/2.5-cm cubes

2 tsp ground cumin

2 tsp dried oregano

2 tbsp lime juice

²/₃ cup dark rum

1 tbsp dark brown sugar

3 garlic cloves, chopped finely

1 large onion, chopped

1 medium red bell pepper, seeded and sliced into rings

1 medium green bell pepper, seeded and sliced into rings

1 medium yellow bell pepper, seeded and sliced into rings

5 cups fish bouillon

2 cups long-grain rice

salt and pepper

crusty bread, to serve

to garnish
fresh oregano leaves
lime wedges

NUTRITION

Calories *547*; Sugars *9 g*; Protein *27 g*; Carbohydrate *85 g*; Fat *4 g*; Saturates *1 g*

 moderate

 35 mins

35 mins

1 Place the cubes of fish in a bowl and add the cumin, oregano, salt, pepper, lime juice, rum, and sugar. Season to taste with salt and pepper. Mix well, cover with plastic wrap, and let chill in the refrigerator for about 2 hours.

2 Meanwhile, place the garlic, onion, and bell peppers in a large pan. Pour in the bouillon and stir in the rice. Bring to a boil over medium heat, then reduce the heat, cover and cook for 15 minutes.

3 Gently add the fish and the marinade juices to the pan. Bring back to a boil and let simmer, uncovered, stirring occasionally, but taking care not to break up the fish, for 10 minutes, until the fish is cooked and the rice is tender.

4 Season to taste with salt and pepper and transfer to a warmed serving plate. Garnish with fresh oregano and lime wedges and serve with bread.

🍳 COOK'S TIP

When buying dried spices and herbs, buy in small quantities and store in a cool dark place in order to preserve their flavor.

This is a rich French stew of fish and vegetables, flavored with saffron and herbs. Traditionally, the fish and vegetables, and the soup, are served separately.

Cotriade

1 Using a mortar and pestle, crush the saffron and add to the fish bouillon. Stir and let stand for at least 10 minutes.

2 Heat the olive oil and butter together in a large pan over low heat. Add the onion and cook gently for 4–5 minutes until softened. Add the garlic, leek, fennel, and potatoes. Cover and cook for another 10–15 minutes until the vegetables are softened.

3 Add the wine and let simmer rapidly for 3–4 minutes until reduced by half. Add the thyme, bay leaves, and tomatoes and stir well. Add the saffron-infused fish bouillon. Bring to a boil, cover and let simmer gently for about 15 minutes until the vegetables are tender.

4 Add the fish, return to a boil and let simmer for another 3–4 minutes until all the fish is tender. Add the parsley and season to taste with salt and pepper. Using a draining spoon, remove the fish and vegetables to a warmed serving dish and garnish with a few sprigs of fresh dill and lemon slices. Serve immediately.

SERVES 6

large pinch of saffron strands
2½ cups hot fish bouillon
1 tbsp olive oil
2 tbsp butter
1 onion, sliced
2 garlic cloves, chopped
1 leek, sliced
1 small fennel bulb, sliced finely
1 lb/450 g potatoes, peeled
    and cut into chunks
⅔ cup dry white wine
1 tbsp fresh thyme leaves
2 bay leaves
4 ripe tomatoes, peeled and chopped
2 lb/900 g mixed fish such as haddock, hake,
    mackerel, red mullet, chopped coarsely
2 tbsp chopped fresh parsley
salt and pepper

to garnish
fresh dill sprigs
lemon slices

NUTRITION
Calories *81*; Sugars *0.9 g*; Protein *7.4 g*;
Carbohydrate *3.8 g*; Fat *3.9 g*; Saturates *1.1 g*

 moderate

 45 mins

45 mins

 COOK'S TIP

Once the fish and vegetables have been cooked, you could process the soup and pass it through a strainer to give a smooth fish soup.

The combination of herrings, apples, and potatoes is popular throughout northern Europe. In salads, one often sees the addition of beets.

Herring *and* Potato Pie

SERVES 4

1 tbsp Dijon mustard
½ cup butter, softened
1 lb/450 g herrings, filleted
1 lb 10 oz/450 g potatoes, peeled
1 large onion, sliced
2 cooking apples, sliced thinly
1 tsp chopped fresh sage
2½ cups hot fish bouillon (to come halfway up the sides of the dish)
1 cup crustless ciabatta bread crumbs
salt and pepper
fresh parsley sprigs, to garnish

NUTRITION
Calories *574*; Sugars *10 g*; Protein *17 g*;
Carbohydrate *48 g*; Fat *36 g*; Saturates *19 g*

 easy

 50 mins

1 hr

1 Mix the mustard with 2 tablespoons of the butter until smooth. Spread this mixture over the cut sides of the herring fillets. Season to taste with salt and pepper and roll up the fillets. Set aside. Generously grease a 9-inch/ 23-cm pie pan with some of the remaining butter.

2 Thinly slice the potatoes, using a mandolin if possible. Bring a large pan of lightly salted water to a boil over medium heat. Add the potatoes and blanch for 3 minutes until just tender. Drain well, refresh under cold running water and pat dry with paper towels.

3 Heat 2 tablespoons of the remaining butter in a skillet over low heat. Add the onion and cook gently for 8–10 minutes until softened, but not colored. Remove from the heat and set aside.

4 Put half the potato slices into the bottom of the prepared pie pan with some seasoning, then add half the apple and half the onion. Put the herring fillets on top of the onion and sprinkle with the sage. Repeat the layers in reverse order, ending with potato slices. Season well with salt and pepper and add the hot bouillon.

5 Melt the remaining butter and stir in the bread crumbs until well combined. Sprinkle the bread crumbs over the pie. Bake in a preheated oven, 375°F/190°C, for 40–50 minutes until the bread crumbs are golden and the herrings are cooked through. Garnish with parsley and serve.

As well as being a simple supper dish, this would make a delicious addition to a brunch menu.

Salt Cod Hash

1 Soak the prepared cod in cold water for 2 hours. Drain well. Bring a large pan of water to a boil over medium heat. Add the fish, then remove from the heat and let stand for 10 minutes. Drain the fish on paper towels and flake the flesh with a fork. Set aside. Discard the soaking water.

2 Bring a pan of water to a boil over medium heat. Add the eggs and let simmer for 7–9 minutes from when the water returns to a boil (7 minutes for a slightly soft center, 9 for a firm center). Immediately drain, then plunge the eggs into cold water to stop them cooking. When cool enough to handle, shell the eggs and coarsely chop. Set aside.

3 Heat the olive oil in a large skillet over medium heat. Add the bacon and cook for 4–5 minutes until crisp and browned. Remove with a draining spoon and drain on paper towels. Add the potatoes to the skillet with the garlic and cook for 8–10 minutes until crisp and golden.

4 Toast the bread on both sides until golden. Drizzle with a little olive oil and set aside.

5 Add the plum tomatoes, bacon, fish, vinegar, and reserved chopped egg to the potatoes and garlic. Cook for another 2 minutes. Stir in the parsley and season to taste with salt and pepper. Put the toast onto 4 serving plates and top with the cod hash. Garnish with chopped parsley and lemon wedges and serve immediately.

SERVES 4

½ quantity Home-Salted Cod (see page 69)
4 eggs
3 tbsp olive oil, plus extra for drizzling
8 bacon, slices chopped
1 lb 9 oz/700 g old potatoes, peeled and diced
8 garlic cloves
8 thick slices good-quality white bread
2 plum tomatoes, peeled and chopped
2 tsp red wine vinegar
2 tbsp chopped fresh parsley plus extra to garnish
salt and pepper
lemon wedges, to garnish

NUTRITION
Calories 857; Sugars 5 g; Protein 58 g; Carbohydrate 82 g; Fat 36 g; Saturates 10 g

 easy

 50 hrs 10 mins

30 mins

Traditionally, a pizza topped with mixed seafood would have no cheese but in this case it helps to protect the fish from overcooking as well as adding texture.

Pizza Marinara

SERVES 4

2 cups all-purpose flour, plus extra for dusting
1 tsp salt
1 package easy-blend yeast
2 tbsp. olive oil, plus extra for oiling
²/₃ cup lukewarm water

tomato sauce

2 tbsp olive oil
1 small onion, chopped finely
1 garlic clove, crushed
14 oz/400 g canned chopped tomatoes
1 tsp dried oregano
1 tbsp tomato paste
salt and pepper

mixed seafood

16 live mussels, scrubbed and bearded
16 large live clams, scrubbed
1 tbsp olive oil
12 raw jumbo shrimp
8 oz/225 g cleaned squid, cut into rings
5½ oz/150 g mozzarella cheese, sliced
olive oil, for drizzling
handful of fresh basil leaves

NUTRITION

Calories *638*; Sugars *5 g*; Protein *55 g*;
Carbohydrate *50 g*; Fat *26 g*; Saturates *11 g*

★★★   moderate

1 hr 15 mins

25 mins

1 To make the pizza base, mix the flour, salt, and yeast together in a large bowl. Add the olive oil and enough water to make a soft, firm dough. Knead on a floured counter for 5 minutes until smooth and elastic.

2 Form the dough into a neat ball and drop into an oiled bowl. Lightly oil the top of the dough, Cover with a clean dishtowel and let rise in a warm place for about 1 hour or until doubled in bulk.

3 Meanwhile, make the sauce. Heat the olive oil in a pan over medium heat. Add the onion and cook for 5 minutes until softened. Add the garlic and cook for a few seconds. Add the tomatoes, oregano, tomato paste, and seasoning. Bring to a boil and let simmer, uncovered, for 30 minutes until thick. Let cool.

4 Put the mussels and clams in a pan with only the water that clings to their shells. Cover and cook over high heat for 3–4 minutes until the shells have opened. Discard any that remain closed. Strain and discard the cooking liquid. Remove the seafood from their shells and set aside.

5 Heat the olive oil in a skillet over medium heat. Add the shrimp and squid and cook for 2–3 minutes until the shrimp have turned pink and the squid is firm.

6 Put several baking sheets into a preheated oven, 450°F/230°C. Knock back the dough and divide into 2. Shape into 10-inch/4-cm rounds. Put onto floured baking sheets. Spread half the sauce on each pizza and add the seafood. Season and top with the cheese. Drizzle with olive oil and sit the sheets on top of the preheated sheets. Cook until golden, then sprinkle with basil and serve.

This is a variation of Pissaladière, the classic French tart of slow-cooked onions on a bread base, very like a pizza.

Onion *and* Tuna Tart

1 To make the topping, heat the butter and oil in a large pan over very low heat. Add the onions. Stir well and cook, covered, for 20 minutes. Add the sugar and salt and cook, covered, for 30–40 minutes, stirring until collapsed and starting to brown. Uncover and cook for another 15–10 minutes until evenly golden. Remove from the heat, stir in the thyme and season to taste with salt and pepper.

2 Meanwhile, make the base. Mix the flour, salt, and yeast together in a large bowl. Add the oil and enough water to make a soft dough that leaves the sides of the bowl clean. Knead the dough on a lightly floured counter for about 5 minutes until smooth and elastic.

3 Form the dough into a neat ball and drop into a lightly oiled bowl. Lightly oil the top of the dough, cover with a clean dishtowel and let rise in a warm place for about 1 hour or until doubled in bulk.

4 Put a baking sheet in a preheated oven, 425°F/220°C. Knock back the risen dough by punching down the center with your fist. Place on the counter and knead briefly. Roll out the dough to fit a lightly oiled Swiss roll pan measuring 13 x 9 inches/33 x/23 cm, leaving a rim. You may have to stretch the dough to fit the pan as it is very springy.

5 Spread the onions in an even layer over the dough. Flake the tuna and put on top of the onions. Arrange the olives over the tuna and season with pepper. Transfer the pan to the preheated baking sheet and cook for about 20 minutes until the dough is golden. Serve immediately.

SERVES 4

2 cups all-purpose flour, plus
    extra for dusting
1 tsp salt
1 package easy-blend yeast
2 tbsp olive oil, plus extra for oiling
⅔ cup lukewarm water

topping
¼ cup butter
2 tbsp olive oil
9 oz/250 g onions, sliced finely
1 tsp sugar
1 tsp salt
1 tsp fresh thyme leaves
7 oz/200 g canned tuna, drained
¼ cup pitted black olives
salt and pepper

NUTRITION
Calories *541*; Sugars *14 g*; Protein *22 g*;
Carbohydrate *61 g*; Fat *25 g*; Saturates *9 g*

  moderate

 1 hr 30 mins

2 hrs

This is a delicious seafood variation of a classic Cornish turnover. Choose any firm white fish, such as cod, and serve hot or cold with crisp salad greens.

Fish Turnover

SERVES 4

4 cups self-rising flour, plus extra for dusting
pinch of salt
1¼ cups butter, diced, plus extra for greasing
2–3 tbsp cold water
1 egg, beaten lightly

filling

¼ cup butter
3 oz/85 g leek, diced
3 oz/85 g onion, chopped finely
3 oz/85 g carrot, diced
8 oz/85 g potato, peeled and diced
12 oz/350 g firm white fish, cut into
    1-inch/2.5-cm pieces
4 tsp white wine vinegar
1 oz/25 g sharp cheese, grated
1 tsp chopped fresh tarragon
salt and pepper

to serve

mixed salad greens
cherry tomatoes, halved

NUTRITION

Calories *250*; Sugars *1.2 g*; Protein *7 g*;
Carbohydrate *23.5 g*; Fat *15 g*; Saturates *9.4 g*

✪✪✪   moderate

🕑   40 mins

🕐   35 mins

1 Strain the flour and salt together into a large bowl. Add the butter and rub it in with your fingertips until the mixture resembles coarse bread crumbs. Add enough cold water to form a dough. Knead briefly until smooth. Wrap in plastic wrap and let chill in the refrigerator for 30 minutes.

2 To make the filling, melt half the butter in a large skillet over low heat. Add the leek, onion, and carrot and cook for 7–8 minutes until the vegetables are softened. Remove from the heat, set aside and let cool slightly.

3 Put the vegetable mixture into a large bowl and add the potato, fish, vinegar, remaining butter, cheese, tarragon, and salt and pepper. Set aside.

4 Remove the dough from the refrigerator and roll out thinly. Using a cutter, press out four 7½-inch/19-cm disks. Alternatively, use a plate of a similar size. Divide the filling among the 4 disks. Moisten the edges of the dough and fold over. Pinch to seal. Crimp the edges and place the pasties on a lightly greased baking sheet. Brush generously with the beaten egg, avoiding the base of the dough to prevent the pasties sticking to it.

5 Bake in a preheated oven, 400°F/200°C, for 15 minutes. Remove from the oven and brush again with the egg glaze. Return to the oven for another 20 minutes. Serve with mixed salad greens and tomatoes.

Buckwheat flour is traditionally used in Breton pancakes. It is available from large supermarkets and health food stores.

Buckwheat Pancakes *with* Smoked Salmon

1 For the filling, mix the crème fraîche, capers, scallions, chile, dill, chives, lemon rind, and seasoning together in a small bowl and set aside.

2 To make the buckwheat pancakes, strain the flours and salt together into a large bowl. Make a well in the center and add the eggs. Mix the milk and water together and add half this mixture to the flour and eggs. Mix until smooth. Gradually add the remaining milk until you have a smooth batter. Stir in the melted butter.

3 Heat an 8-inch/20-cm skillet over medium heat. Dip a piece of wadded paper towel into a little vegetable oil and rub this over the surface of the skillet to give a thin coating. Ladle about 2 tablespoons of pancake mixture into the skillet, tilting and shaking the skillet to coat the bottom evenly. Cook for 1 minute until the edges start to lift away from the skillet. Using a palette knife, lift the pancake and turn it over. It should be pale golden. Cook for 30 seconds on the second side. Remove from the skillet and place on a warmed plate. Re-grease and reheat the skillet and repeat with the remaining mixture to make 12–14 pancakes, depending on their thickness.

4 Place a slice of smoked salmon on each pancake and top with 2 teaspoons of the crème fraîche mixture. Fold the pancake in half and then in half again to form a triangle. Transfer to 4 serving plates, garnish with lemon slices and a few sprigs of fresh dill and serve.

SERVES 4

½ cup all-purpose flour
½ cup buckwheat flour
pinch of salt
2 large eggs
¾ cup milk
scant ½ cup water
2 tbsp butter, melted
4 tbsp vegetable oil, for cooking
lemon slices and dill sprigs, to garnish

filling
½ cup crème fraîche, or mascarpone cheese
1 tbsp capers, drained, rinsed, and roughly chopped
3 scallions, chopped finely
1 fresh red chile, seeded and finely chopped
1 tbsp chopped fresh dill, plus extra fresh dill sprigs to garnish
1 tbsp chopped fresh chives
1 tsp lemon rind
8 oz/225 g sliced smoked salmon
salt and pepper

NUTRITION
Calories *385*; Sugars *4 g*; Protein *24 g*; Carbohydrate *27 g*; Fat *21 g*; Saturates *9 g*

★★★   moderate

25 mins

25 mins

This is a typical Chinese
breakfast dish, although it
is probably best served as
a lunch or supper dish at
a Western table!

Crab Congee

SERVES 4

generous 1 cup short-grain rice
6¼ cups fish bouillon
½ tsp salt
3½ oz/100 g Chinese sausage, sliced thinly
8 oz/225 g white crabmeat
6 scallions, sliced
2 tbsp chopped fresh cilantro
pepper, to serve

1 Place the short-grain rice in a large preheated wok or skillet.

2 Add the bouillon to the wok or skillet and bring to a boil over medium heat.

3 Reduce the heat, then let simmer gently for 1 hour, stirring occasionally.

4 Add the salt, sliced Chinese sausage, white crabmeat, sliced scallions, and chopped cilantro to the wok and heat through for about 5 minutes.

5 Add a little more water to the wok if the congee "porridge" is too thick, stirring well.

6 Transfer the crab congee to 4 warmed serving bowls, sprinkle with freshly ground black pepper and serve immediately.

NUTRITION
Calories 327; Sugars 0.1 g; Protein 18 g;
Carbohydrate 50 g; Fat 7 g; Saturates 2 g

 easy

 35 mins

35 mins

1 hr 15 mins

 COOK'S TIP

If using fresh crab, always choose crabs that are heavy for their size and that do not sound watery when shaken.

This combination of assorted seafood and tender vegetables flavored with ginger makes an ideal light meal when served with thread noodles.

Seafood Stir-Fry

1 Bring a small pan of water to a boil over medium heat. Add the asparagus and blanch for 1–2 minutes.

2 Drain the asparagus, set aside and keep warm.

3 Heat the corn oil in a preheated wok or large skillet over medium heat. Add the ginger, leek, carrots, and baby corn and cook for about 3 minutes. Do not let the vegetables brown.

4 Add the soy sauce, oyster sauce, and honey to the wok or skillet.

5 Stir in the cooked shellfish and stir-fry for 2–3 minutes until the vegetables are just tender and the shellfish are thoroughly heated through. Add the blanched asparagus and stir-fry for about 2 minutes.

6 To serve, pile the cooked noodles onto 4 warmed serving plates and spoon the seafood and vegetable stir-fry over them.

7 Garnish with the cooked shrimp and snipped chives and serve immediately.

SERVES 4

3½ oz/100 g small, thin asparagus spears, trimmed
1 tbsp corn oil
1-inch/2.5-cm piece of fresh gingerroot, cut into thin strips
1 leek, shredded
2 carrots, cut into very thin strips
3½ oz/100 g baby corn cobs, cut into fourths lengthwise
2 tbsp light soy sauce
1 tbsp oyster sauce
1 tsp honey
1 lb/450 g cooked, assorted shellfish, thawed if frozen
freshly cooked egg noodles, to serve

to garnish
4 cooked jumbo shrimp
small bunch of snipped fresh chives

NUTRITION
Calories *226*; Sugars *5 g*; Protein *35 g*; Carbohydrate *6 g*; Fat *7 g*; Saturates *1 g*

 moderate

5 mins

15 mins

Delicately scented with sesame, lime, and cilantro, these noodles make an unusual lunch or supper dish.

Sesame Noodles *with* Shrimp

SERVES 4

1 garlic clove, chopped
1 scallion, chopped
1 small, fresh red chile, seeded and sliced
1 tsp chopped fresh cilantro
10½ oz/300 g dried fine egg noodles
2 tbsp vegetable oil
2 tsp sesame oil
1 tsp shrimp paste
8 oz/225 g raw shrimp, peeled
2 tbsp lime juice
2 tbsp Thai fish sauce
1 tsp sesame seeds, toasted

1 Place the garlic, onion, chile, and cilantro into a mortar and grind to a smooth paste with a pestle.

2 Bring a pan of water to a boil over medium heat. Add the noodles and cook for 4 minutes or according to the package directions.

3 Meanwhile, heat the oils in a preheated wok or large, heavy-based skillet over medium-high heat. Stir in the shrimp paste and cilantro mixture, and stir-fry for 1 minute.

4 Add the shrimp and stir-fry for 2 minutes. Stir in the lime juice and Thai fish sauce and stir-fry for another 1 minute.

5 Drain the noodles and add them into the wok, tossing well. Sprinkle with the sesame seeds and serve immediately.

NUTRITION
Calories *430*; Sugars *2 g*; Protein *23 g*;
Carbohydrate *56 g*; Fat *15 g*; Saturates *3 g*

 easy
 5 mins
5 10 mins

(cook) **COOK'S TIP**

The roots of cilantro are widely used in Thai cooking, so if you can obtain fresh cilantro with the root attached, use the whole plant in this dish for maximum flavor. If not, use stems as well as the leaves.

This dish makes a delicious light lunch in a matter of minutes and would be a quick and easy midweek supper when served with salad greens.

Rice Noodles *with* Spinach

1 Soak the rice noodles in hot water for 15 minutes, or according to the package directions, then drain well.

2 Soak the shrimp in a bowl of hot water for 10 minutes and drain well. Wash the spinach thoroughly, drain well and remove any tough stems.

3 Heat the peanut oil in a preheated wok or large skillet over medium heat. Add the garlic and cook for 1 minute. Stir in the green curry paste and cook for 30 seconds. Stir in the soaked shrimp and stir-fry for 30 seconds.

4 Add the spinach and stir-fry for 1–2 minutes or until just wilted.

5 Stir in the sugar and soy sauce, then add the noodles and toss thoroughly to mix evenly. Transfer to 4 warmed serving bowls and serve immediately.

SERVES 4

4 oz/115 g thin rice stick noodles
2 tbsp dried shrimp, optional
4 cups fresh young spinach
1 tbsp peanut oil
2 garlic cloves, chopped finely
2 tsp Thai green curry paste
1 tsp sugar
1 tbsp light soy sauce

NUTRITION
Calories *159*; Sugars *3 g*; Protein *8 g*;
Carbohydrate *27 g*; Fat *2 g*; Saturates *0 g*

  easy

20 mins

6–8 mins

COOK'S TIP

Young, tender spinach leaves, which cook in seconds, are best for this dish. If you use older spinach, shred the leaves before adding to the dish, so they cook more quickly.

This is the ideal dish when you have unexpected guests because the parcels are quick to prepare, but look fantastic.

Pasta *and* Shrimp Parcels

SERVES 4

1 lb/450 g dried fettuccine
²/₃ cup pesto
4 tsp extra virgin olive oil
1 lb 10 oz/750 g large raw shrimp, peeled and deveined
2 garlic cloves, minced
½ cup dry white wine
salt and pepper

1 Cut out four 12-inch/30-cm squares of waxed paper.

2 Bring a large pan of lightly salted water to a boil over medium heat. Add the fettuccine and cook for 2–3 minutes, until just softened. Drain and set aside.

3 Mix together the fettuccine and half of the pesto together. Spread out the paper squares and put 1 teaspoon of olive oil in the center of each. Divide the fettuccine among the the squares, then divide the shrimp and place on top of the fettuccine.

4 Mix the remaining pesto together with the garlic and spoon it over the shrimp. Season each parcel with salt and pepper and sprinkle with the wine.

5 Dampen the edges of the waxed paper and wrap the parcels loosely, twisting the edges to seal.

6 Place the parcels on a large cookie sheet and bake in a preheated oven, 400°F/200°C, for 10–15 minutes. Transfer the parcels to 4 serving plates and serve immediately.

NUTRITION
Calories *640*; Sugars *1 g*; Protein *50 g*;
Carbohydrate *42 g*; Fat *29 g*; Saturates *4 g*

moderate
15 mins
25 mins

🍳 **COOK'S TIP**

Traditionally, these parcels are designed to look like little money bags. The resemblance is more effective with waxed paper than with foil.

Fish and fruit are tossed with a trio of bell peppers in this spicy dish, which can be served with noodles for a quick, healthy meal.

Noodles *with* Cod *and* Mango

1 Place the egg noodles in a large bowl and pour over enough boiling water to cover. Let stand for about 10 minutes.

2 Place the cod in a large bowl. Add the paprika and toss well to coat the fish.

3 Heat the corn oil in a preheated wok or large, heavy-based skillet over medium heat.

4 Add the onion, orange, red, and green bell peppers, and baby corn cobs to the wok and cook for about 5 minutes.

5 Add the cod to the wok with the mango and cook for another 2–3 minutes or until the fish is tender.

6 Add the bean sprouts to the wok and toss well to combine.

7 Mix the tomato catsup, soy sauce, sherry, and cornstarch together. Add the mixture to the wok and cook, stirring occasionally, until the juices thicken.

8 Drain the noodles well and transfer to 4 warmed serving bowls. Transfer the cod and mango stir-fry to separate serving bowls. Serve immediately.

SERVES 4

9 oz/250 g dried egg noodles
1 lb/450 g skinless cod fillet, cut into
    thin strips
1 tbsp paprika
2 tbsp corn oil
1 red onion, sliced
1 orange bell pepper, seeded and sliced
1 red bell pepper, seeded and sliced
1 green bell pepper, seeded and sliced
3½ oz/100 g baby corn cobs,
    halved lengthwise
1 mango, peeled, pitted, and sliced
1 cup bean sprouts
2 tbsp tomato catsup
2 tbsp soy sauce
2 tbsp medium sherry
1 tsp cornstarch

NUTRITION
Calories *274*; Sugars *11 g*; Protein *25 g*;
Carbohydrate *26 g*; Fat *8 g*; Saturates *1 g*

✪✪✪   moderate
         10 mins
         25 mins

This is another tempting seafood dish where the eye is delighted as much as the taste buds.

Baked Scallops *with* Pasta *in* Shells

SERVES 4

12 scallops
3 tbsp olive oil
3 cups small, dried whole-wheat pasta shells
⅝ cup Fresh Fish Bouillon (see page 14)
1 onion, chopped
juice and finely grated rind of 2 lemons
⅝ cup heavy cream
2 cups grated hard cheese
salt and pepper

to serve
lime wedges
crusty brown bread

NUTRITION
Calories 725; Sugars 2 g; Protein 38 g;
Carbohydrate 38 g; Fat 48 g; Saturates 25 g

moderate

20 mins

30 mins

1 Remove the scallops from their shells. Scrape off the skirt and the black intestinal thread. Set aside the white part (the flesh) and the orange part (the coral or roe). Very carefully ease the flesh and coral from the shell with a short, but very strong knife.

2 Wash the shells under cold running water and dry them well with paper towels. Put the shells on a cookie sheet, sprinkle lightly with two-thirds of the olive oil and set aside.

3 Meanwhile, bring a large pan of lightly salted water to a boil over medium heat. Add the pasta shells and 1 teaspoon of the olive oil and cook according to the package directions or until tender, but still firm to the bite. Drain and spoon 1 oz/25 g of pasta into each scallop shell.

4 Put the scallops, bouillon and onion into an ovenproof dish and season with pepper to taste. Cover with foil and bake in a preheated oven, 350°F/180°C, for 8 minutes.

5 Remove from the oven and use a draining spoon to transfer the scallops to the shells. Add 1 tablespoon of the cooking liquid to each shell, along with with a drizzle of lemon juice, lemon rind, and cream. Top with the cheese.

6 Increase the oven temperature to 450°F/230°C and return the scallops to the oven for another 4 minutes. Serve the scallops in their shells with lime wedges and crusty brown bread.

A combination of hard cider, apple juice, and tarragon vinegar gives mouthwatering flavor to this warming dish.

Spaghetti *alla* Bucaniera

1 Season the flour with salt and pepper. Sprinkle ¼ cup of the seasoned flour onto a shallow plate. Press the fish pieces into the seasoned flour until they are thoroughly coated.

2 Melt the butter in an ovenproof casserole over low heat. Add the fish fillets, shallots, garlic, carrot, and leek, and cook, stirring frequently, for 10 minutes.

3 Sprinkle over the remaining seasoned flour and cook, stirring constantly, for 2 minutes. Gradually stir in the hard cider, apple juice, anchovy paste, and tarragon vinegar. Bring to a boil and let simmer for 35 minutes. Alternatively, bake the fish in a preheated oven, 350°F/180°C, for 30 minutes.

4 About 15 minutes before the end of the cooking time, bring a large pan of lightly salted water to a boil over medium heat. Add the spaghetti and olive oil and cook for about 12 minutes or until tender, but still firm to the bite. Drain well and transfer to a large serving dish.

5 Arrange the fish on top of the spaghetti and pour over the sauce. Garnish with chopped parsley and serve immediately.

SERVES 4

¾ cup all-purpose flour
1 lb/450 g brill or sole fillets, skinned and chopped
1 lb/450 g hake fillets, skinned and chopped
6 tbsp butter
4 shallots, chopped finely
2 garlic cloves, crushed
1 carrot, diced
1 leek, chopped finely
1¼ cups hard cider
1¼ cups apple juice
2 tsp anchovy paste
1 tbsp tarragon vinegar
1 lb/450 g dried spaghetti
1 tsp olive oil
salt and pepper
chopped fresh parsley, to garnish

NUTRITION
Calories *588*; Sugars *5 g*; Protein *36 g*; Carbohydrate *68 g*; Fat *18 g*; Saturates *9 g*

 moderate

25 mins

 50 mins

🍳 **COOK'S TIP**

Flavored vinegars are easy to make yourself. Simply place a few sprigs of fresh herbs into a bottle of white wine vinegar. Screw down tightly and leave in a cool dark place for 2–3 weeks before using.

This quick, easy, and inexpensive dish would be ideal for an everyday family supper and will quickly become a firm favorite.

Smoked Haddock Casserole

SERVES 4

2 tbsp butter, plus extra for greasing
1 lb/450 g smoked haddock fillets, cut into
    4 slices
2½ cups milk
scant ¼ cup all-purpose flour
pinch of freshly grated nutmeg
3 tbsp heavy cream
1 tbsp chopped fresh parsley
2 eggs, hard-cooked and mashed to a pulp
4 cups dried fusilli
1 tbsp lemon juice
salt and pepper
fresh flatleaf parsley sprigs, to garnish

to serve
boiled new potatoes
freshly cooked beets

1 Thoroughly grease a casserole with a little butter. Put the haddock into the casserole and pour over the milk. Bake in a preheated oven, 400°F/200°C, for about 15 minutes or until tender and the flesh flakes easily.

2 Carefully pour the cooking liquid into a pitcher without breaking up the fish. Leave the fish in the casserole.

3 Melt the butter in a pan over low heat. Stir in the flour, then gradually whisk in the reserved cooking liquid. Season to taste with salt, pepper, and nutmeg. Stir in the cream, parsley, and mashed eggs and cook, stirring constantly, for 2 minutes.

4 Meanwhile, bring a large pan of lightly salted water to a boil over medium heat. Add the fusilli and the lemon juice, return to a boil and cook for about 8–10 minutes until tender, but still firm to the bite.

5 Drain the pasta and spoon or tip it over the fish. Top with the egg sauce and return the casserole to the oven for 10 minutes.

6 Transfer the casserole to 4 large serving plates, garnish with a few sprigs of fresh parsley and serve with boiled new potatoes and beets.

NUTRITION
Calories *525*; Sugars *8 g*; Protein *41 g*;
Carbohydrate *53 g*; Fat *18 g*; Saturates *10 g*

⊛⊛⊛   moderate
🕐   20 mins
🕐   40 mins

COOK'S TIP

You can use any type of dried pasta for this casserole. Try penne, conchiglie, farfalle, or rigatoni.

This dish is ideal for a substantial supper. You can use whatever pasta you like, but the tricolor varieties will give the most colorful results.

Shrimp Pasta Bake

1 Bring a large pan of lightly salted water to a boil over medium heat. Add the pasta and cook for 8–10 minutes or until tender, but still firm to the bite. Drain well.

2 Meanwhile, heat the vegetable oil in a large skillet over low heat. Add the mushrooms and all but a handful of the scallions and cook, stirring frequently, for 4–5 minutes until softened.

3 Place the cooked pasta in a large bowl and mix in the mushroom and scallion mixture, tuna, and shrimp.

4 Blend the cornstarch with a little milk to make a paste. Pour the remaining milk into a pan and stir in the paste. Heat, stirring constantly, until the sauce starts to thicken. Season well with salt and pepper. Add the sauce to the pasta mixture. Transfer to an ovenproof gratin dish and place on a large cookie sheet.

5 Arrange the tomato slices over the pasta and sprinkle with the bread crumbs and grated cheese. Bake in a preheated oven, 375°F/190°C, for about 25–30 minutes until golden. Sprinkle with the reserved scallions and serve.

SERVES 4

3 cups dried tricolor pasta shapes
1 tbsp vegetable oil
2½ cups sliced white mushrooms
1 bunch of scallions, trimmed and chopped
14 oz/400 g canned tuna in brine, drained and flaked
6 oz/175 g peeled shrimp, thawed if frozen
2 tbsp cornstarch
1¾ cups skim milk
4 tomatoes, sliced thinly
½ cup fresh bread crumbs
¼ cup grated reduced-fat sharp cheese
salt and pepper

NUTRITION
Calories 723; Sugars 9 g; Protein 56 g; Carbohydrate 114 g; Fat 8 g; Saturates 2 g

✪✪✪✪ challenging

 10 mins

 50 mins

Entertaining

Fish and shellfish are ideal for entertaining. They are perceived as being more exotic than many meat dishes and yet are often easier to prepare. Shellfish in particular is thought to be luxurious, but nowadays it is readily available and reasonably priced.

The recipes in this chapter have been designed for those occasions when you really want to make an impression. There should be something here for every budget, ability, and taste, from Stuffed Monkfish Tail, and Crab Soufflé, to Hot-Smoked Trout Tart, and Spinach Roulade.

There are more traditional dishes, such as Luxury Fish Pie and Sole Florentine, as well as more exciting-sounding dishes such as Cuttlefish in Their Own Ink.

Skate has a strong flavor that makes it a rich fish. It is perfect partnered with this sauce, which is sharp in flavor. Serve it with boiled new potatoes and green beans.

Skate *with* Black Butter

SERVES 4

2 lb/900 g skate wings, cut into 4 pieces
¾ cup butter
¾ cup red wine vinegar
½ oz/15 g capers, drained
1 tbsp chopped fresh parsley
salt and pepper

court-bouillon

3¾ cups cold water
3¾ cups dry white wine
3 tbsp white wine vinegar
2 large carrots, chopped coarsely
1 onion, chopped coarsely
2 celery sticks, chopped coarsely
2 leeks, chopped coarsely
2 garlic cloves, chopped coarsely
2 bay leaves
4 fresh parsley sprigs
4 fresh thyme sprigs
6 black peppercorns

to serve

boiled new potatoes
freshly cooked green beans

NUTRITION

Calories *381*; Sugars *0 g*; Protein *34 g*;
Carbohydrate *0 g*; Fat *27 g*; Saturates *17 g*

easy

20 mins

1 hr 30 mins

1 Start by making the court-bouillon. Put all of the ingredients into a large pan, along with 1 teaspoon of salt and bring slowly to a boil over low heat. Cover and let simmer gently for 30 minutes. Strain the liquid through a fine strainer into a clean pan. Bring to a boil again and let simmer rapidly, uncovered, for 15–20 minutes, until reduced to 2½ cups.

2 Place the skate in a wide shallow pan and pour over the court-bouillon. Bring to a boil over low heat and let simmer very gently for 15 minutes, or a little longer depending on the thickness of the skate. Drain the fish, set aside and keep warm.

3 Meanwhile, melt the butter in a skillet over medium heat. Cook until the butter changes color to a dark brown and smells very nutty.

4 Add the vinegar, capers, and parsley and let simmer for 1 minute. Pour over the fish. Serve with plenty of boiled new potatoes and green beans.

Sole à la Meunière, or "miller's wife style," gets its name from the light dusting of flour that the fish is given before frying.

Sole *à la* Meunière

1 Mix the flour with the salt and place on a large plate or tray. Drop the fish into the flour, one at a time, and shake well to remove any excess. Melt 3 tablespoons of the butter in a small pan over low heat and use to liberally brush the fish all over.

2 Place the fish under a preheated hot broiler and cook for about 5 minutes on each side.

3 Meanwhile, melt the remaining butter in a pan over low heat. Pour cold water into a bowl, large enough to take the bottom of the pan. Keep nearby.

4 Heat the butter until it turns a golden brown and starts to smell nutty. Remove immediately from the heat and immerse the bottom of the pan in the cold water to stop the cooking.

5 Put the fish onto 4 large serving plates, drizzle with the lemon juice and sprinkle with the parsley and preserved lemon (if using). Pour over the browned butter and garnish with a few sprigs of fresh parsley and lemon wedges. Serve immediately.

🍳 **COOK'S TIP**

If you have a large enough skillet you can fry the floured fish in butter, if you prefer.

SERVES 4
½ cup all-purpose flour
1 tsp salt
14 oz/400 g soles, cleaned and skinned
⅔ cup butter
3 tbsp lemon juice
1 tbsp chopped fresh parsley
¼ of a preserved lemon, chopped finely (optional)
salt and pepper

court-bouillon
fresh parsley sprigs
lemon wedges

NUTRITION
Calories 584; Sugars 0 g; Protein 74 g; Carbohydrate 10 g; Fat 29 g; Saturates 14 g

⭐⭐ easy
🕐 20 mins
🕐 15 mins

This dish is a classic combination of rolled sole fillets in a creamy cheese sauce, cooked with spinach. To save time, prepare the cheese sauce in advance.

Sole Florentine

SERVES 4

2½ cups milk
2 strips of lemon rind
2 fresh tarragon sprigs
1 bay leaf
½ onion, sliced
2 tbsp butter, plus extra for greasing
½ cup all-purpose flour
2 tsp mustard powder
3 tbsp freshly grated Parmesan cheese
2¼ cups heavy cream
pinch of freshly grated nutmeg
1 lb/450 g fresh spinach, washed
1 lb 10 oz/750 g sole, quarter-cut fillets
    (2 from each side of the fish)
salt and pepper
crisp salad greens, to serve

NUTRITION

Calories *945*; Sugars *12 g*; Protein *80 g*;
Carbohydrate *23 g*; Fat *59 g*; Saturates *32 g*

 moderate

 45 mins

45 mins

1 Put the milk, lemon rind, tarragon, bay leaf, and onion into a large pan and bring slowly to a boil over low heat. Remove from the heat and let stand for 30 minutes to let the flavors infuse.

2 Melt the butter in a clean pan over low heat. Stir in the flour and mustard powder until smooth. Strain the infused milk, discarding the lemon, herbs, and onion. Gradually beat the milk into the butter and flour mixture until smooth. Bring slowly to a boil, stirring constantly, until thickened. Let simmer for 2 minutes. Remove from the heat and stir in the cheese, cream, nutmeg, and salt and pepper to taste. Cover with plastic wrap and set aside.

3 Lightly grease a large baking dish. Bring a large pan of lightly salted water to a boil over medium heat. Add the spinach and blanch for 30 seconds. Drain and immediately refresh under cold running water. Drain and pat dry with paper towels. Put the spinach in a layer on the bottom of the prepared dish.

4 Wash the fish fillets under cold running water and pat dry with paper towels. Season to taste with salt and pepper and roll up. Arrange on top of the spinach and pour over the sauce. Cook in a preheated oven, 400°F/200°C, for 35 minutes until bubbling and golden. Serve with a salad greens.

COOK'S TIP

For a budget version of this dish, use lemon sole instead of sole.

The beauty of this dish is that the fish cooks alongside a selection of vegetables, which means you need only boil some new potatoes to serve with it.

John Dory *en* Papillote

1 Wash the fish fillets under cold running water and pat dry with paper towels. Set aside. Cut 4 large rectangles of baking parchment measuring 18 x 12 inches/46 x 30 cm. Fold each in half to make a 9 x 12-inch/23 x 30-cm rectangle. Cut this into a large heart shape and open out.

2 Lay 1 John Dory fillet on one half of each paper heart. Top with one quarter of the olives, tomatoes, green beans, and basil, and 1 lemon slice. Drizzle over 1 teaspoon of olive oil and season well with salt and pepper.

3 Fold over the other half of the paper and fold the edges of the paper together to enclose. Repeat to make 4 packets.

4 Place the packets on a large cookie sheet and cook in a preheated oven, 400°F/200°C, for 15 minutes or until the fish is tender.

5 Transfer each packet to a serving plate, unopened, allowing your guests to open their packets and enjoy the wonderful aroma. Suggest that they garnish their portions with fresh basil and serve with a generous helping of boiled new potatoes.

SERVES 4

2 John Dory, filleted
1 cup pitted black olives
12 cherry tomatoes, halved
4 oz/115 g green beans, trimmed
handful of fresh basil leaves
4 fresh lemon slices
4 tsp olive oil
salt and pepper
fresh basil leaves, to garnish
boiled new potatoes, to serve

NUTRITION
Calories *368*; Sugars *2 g*; Protein *49 g*;
Carbohydrate *3 g*; Fat *18 g*; Saturates *3 g*

 easy

 10 mins

15 mins

COOK'S TIP

Try spreading the fish with a little olive paste, some chopped sun-dried tomatoes, a little goat cheese, and fresh basil.

Baby artichokes are slowly cooked with olive oil, garlic, thyme, and lemon to create a soft blend of flavors that harmonize very well with the fish, without overpowering it.

Broiled Sea Bass *with* Artichokes

SERVES 4

4 lb/1.7 kg baby artichokes
2½ tbsp fresh lemon juice, plus the cut halves of the lemon
⅔ cup olive oil
10 garlic cloves, sliced finely
1 tbsp fresh thyme, plus extra to garnish
4 oz/115 g sea bass fillets
1 tbsp olive oil
salt and pepper
crusty bread, to serve

1 Peel away the tough outer leaves of each artichoke until the yellow-green heart is revealed. Slice off the pointed top at about halfway between the point and the top of the stem. Cut off the stem and pare off what is left of the dark green leaves surrounding the bottom of the artichoke.

2 Submerge the prepared artichokes in water containing the cut halves of the lemon to prevent them browning. When all the artichokes have been prepared, turn them choke side down, and slice thinly.

3 Warm the olive oil in a large pan over low heat. Add the sliced artichokes, garlic, thyme, lemon juice, and salt and pepper to taste. Cover and cook for 20–30 minutes, without coloring, until tender.

4 Meanwhile, brush the fish fillets with the remaining olive oil and season well with salt and pepper. Transfer to a lit barbecue or preheated ridged griddle and cook for 3–4 minutes on each side until just tender.

5 Divide the stewed artichokes among serving plates and top each with a sea bass fillet. Garnish with chopped thyme and serve with lots of crusty bread.

NUTRITION
Calories *400*; Sugars *3 g*; Protein *28 g*; Carbohydrate *7 g*; Fat *30 g*; Saturates *5 g*

  easy

  20 mins

  35 mins

COOK'S TIP

If fresh artichokes are unavailable, use canned.

Sea bass is surely the king of round fish, with a delightful flavor and texture. Here it is cooked very simply and served with a highly flavored sauce of ratatouille and a basil dressing.

Sea Bass *with* Ratatouille

1 To make the ratatouille, cut the eggplant and zucchini into chunks about the same size as the onion and bell peppers. Put the eggplant and zucchini into a strainer with the salt and let drain for 30 minutes. Rinse thoroughly and pat dry on paper towels. Set aside.

2 Heat the oil in a large pan over low heat. Add the onion and garlic and cook gently for 10 minutes until softened. Add the bell peppers, eggplant, and zucchini. Season to taste with salt and pepper and stir well. Cover and let simmer very gently for 30 minutes until all the vegetables have softened. Add the tomatoes and cook for another 15 minutes.

3 Meanwhile make the dressing. Put the basil, garlic, and half the olive oil into a food processor and process until finely chopped. Add the remaining olive oil, and lemon juice, and season to taste with salt and pepper.

4 Season the sea bass fillets and brush with a little olive oil. Preheat a skillet until very hot and add the fish, skin side down. Cook for 2–3 minutes until the skin is browned and crispy. Turn the fish over and cook for another 2–3 minutes until just cooked through.

5 To serve, stir the basil into the ratatouille, then transfer to 4 serving plates. Top with the cooked fish and spoon around the dressing, then serve.

SERVES 4

2 large sea bass, filleted
olive oil, for brushing
salt and pepper
ratatouille
1 large eggplant
2 medium zucchini
1 tbsp sea salt
4 tbsp olive oil
1 medium onion, chopped coarsely
2 garlic cloves, crushed
½ red bell pepper, seeded and
    coarsely chopped
½ green bell pepper, seeded and
    coarsely chopped
2 large ripe tomatoes, peeled and chopped
1 tbsp freshly chopped basil
dressing
5 tbsp coarsely chopped fresh basil
2 garlic cloves, chopped coarsely
4 tbsp olive oil
1 tbsp lemon juice
salt and pepper

NUTRITION
Calories *373*; Sugars *9 g*; Protein *42 g*;
Carbohydrate *10 g*; Fat *18 g*; Saturates *3 g*

⭐⭐⭐   moderate
       45 mins
       1 hr

This is a lovely Asian-inspired dish of sea bass, delicately flavored with scallions, ginger, and soy sauce. Be careful pouring the hot oil over the fish and scallions, as it may spit a little.

Whole Sea Bass *with* Ginger

SERVES 4

1 lb 12 oz/800 g whole sea bass, scaled and gutted
4 tbsp light soy sauce
5 scallions, cut into long, fine shreds
2 tbsp finely shredded fresh ginger
4 tbsp fresh cilantro leaves
5 tsp corn oil
1 tsp sesame oil
4 tbsp hot fish bouillon, made from a bouillon cube
lime wedges, to garnish
steamed rice, to serve

1 Wash the fish under cold running water and pat dry with paper towels. Brush with 2 tablespoons of the soy sauce. Sprinkle half the scallions and all the ginger over a steaming tray or large plate and put the fish on top.

2 Half fill a large pan with water and fit a steamer on top. Bring the water to a boil over medium heat. Put the steaming plate with the sea bass into the steamer and cover with a tight-fitting lid. Keeping the water boiling, steam the fish for 10–12 minutes until tender.

3 Carefully remove the plate and lift the fish onto a serving plate, leaving behind the scallions and ginger. Sprinkle over the remaining scallions and cilantro leaves.

4 Put the corn oil into a small pan and heat until almost smoking. Add the sesame oil and immediately pour over the fish and scallions. Mix the remaining soy sauce with the fish bouillon, then pour over the fish. Garnish with lime wedges and serve immediately with steamed rice.

NUTRITION
Calories *185*; Sugars *1 g*; Protein *31 g*; Carbohydrate *2 g*; Fat *6 g*; Saturates *1 g*

 moderate

 10 mins

10 mins

15 mins

Poached cod has a very delicate flavor. Here it is teamed with a piquant relish of finely diced, colorful vegetables, and served cold.

Cold Poached Cod Steaks

1 Put the carrot, onion, celery, parsley, thyme, garlic, water, and salt into a large pan and bring to a boil over medium heat. Let simmer gently for 10 minutes. Add the fish and poach for 5–7 minutes until just firm in the center. Remove the fish with a draining spoon and let cool. Let chill for 2 hours.

2 Meanwhile, make the pickled vegetable relish. Soak the salted anchovies in several changes of water for 15 minutes, then chop. Mix the carrot, bell pepper, onion, garlic, cornichons, olives, capers, anchovies, vinegar, olive oil, and parsley together in a non-metallic bowl. Season to taste with salt and pepper, adding a little more vinegar or olive oil to taste. Cover and let chill in the refrigerator for 1 hour.

3 To serve, place a cold cod steak on each of 4 serving plates. Spoon the relish over the top. Serve immediately with salad greens.

SERVES 4

1 small carrot, sliced thinly
1 small onion, sliced thinly
1 celery stick, sliced thinly
3 fresh parsley sprigs
3 fresh thyme sprigs
1 garlic clove, sliced
7½ cups water
6 oz/175 g cod steaks

pickled vegetable relish
2 salted anchovies
1 small carrot, diced finely
¼ red bell pepper, seeded and finely diced
½ small red onion, diced finely
1 garlic clove, chopped finely
3 tbsp finely diced cornichon pickles
4 tbsp chopped pitted green olives
1 tbsp capers, drained and rinsed
1 tbsp red wine vinegar
scant ½ cup olive oil
2 tbsp chopped fresh parsley
salt and pepper
salad greens, to serve

NUTRITION
Calories *402*; Sugars *3 g*; Protein *33 g*;
Carbohydrate *4 g*; Fat *28 g*; Saturates *4 g*

✪✪✪ moderate
2 hrs 30 mins
7 mins

 COOK'S TIP

You can also use salmon steaks for this dish, if you prefer.

Cooking the fish in a layer of salt ensures that the flesh stays very moist without becoming salty.

Sea Bream *in a* Salt Crust

SERVES 4

2 lb 4 oz/1 kg whole sea bream
1 shallot, sliced thinly
2 fresh parsley sprigs
1 fresh tarragon sprig
2 garlic cloves, chopped coarsely
4 lb 8 oz–5 lb 8 oz/2–2.5 kg coarse sea salt

lemon butter sauce
2 shallots, chopped very finely
4 tbsp lemon juice
1¼ cold unsalted butter, diced
salt and pepper

to garnish
lemon wedges
fresh herb sprigs

1 Wash the sea bream under cold running water and pat dry with paper towels. Fill the body cavity with the shallot, parsley, tarragon, and garlic, then set aside.

2 Sprinkle a thick layer of salt into the bottom of a roasting pan large enough to hold the fish, with lots of space round it. Top with the fish, then pour the remaining salt over the fish to completely cover it. Sprinkle the water lightly all over the salt. Cook in a preheated oven, 425°F/220°C, for 25 minutes.

3 To make the lemon butter sauce, put the shallots and lemon juice into a pan and let simmer gently over low heat for 5 minutes. Increase the heat until the lemon juice is reduced by half. Reduce the heat and add the butter, piece by piece, whisking constantly, until all the butter is incorporated and the sauce is thick. Season to taste with salt and pepper and keep warm.

4 Remove the fish from the oven and let stand for 5 minutes before cracking open the salt. Remove the fish, garnish with lemon wedges and fresh herbs, then serve with the lemon butter sauce.

NUTRITION
Calories *185*; Sugars *1 g*; Protein *31 g*;
Carbohydrate *2 g*; Fat *6 g*; Saturates *1 g*

 moderate

 10 mins

25 mins

COOK'S TIP

You can also use pure, unperfumed bath salts, if you can find them, rather than the more expensive table salt.

This is a dramatic looking dish due to the inclusion of the cuttlefish ink. Although this is a typically Spanish dish, it has been teamed with polenta as the combination of the dark stew and yellow polenta make a beautiful contrast.

Cuttlefish *in Their Own* Ink

1 To prepare the cuttlefish, cut off the tentacles in front of the eyes and remove the beak-like mouth from the center of the tentacles. Cut the head section from the body and discard it. Cut open the body section from top to bottom along the dark, colored back. Remove the cuttle bone and the entrails, reserving the ink sack. Skin the body. Chop the flesh coarsely and set aside. Split open the ink sack and dilute the ink in a little water. Set aside.

2 Heat the olive oil in a large pan over low heat. Add the onion and cook for 8–10 minutes until softened and starting to brown. Add the garlic and cook for another 30 seconds. Add the cuttlefish and cook for another 5 minutes until starting to brown. Add the paprika and stir for another 30 seconds before adding the tomatoes. Cook for 2–3 minutes until they have collapsed.

3 Add the red wine, fish bouillon, and diluted ink and stir well. Bring to a boil and let simmer gently, uncovered, for 25 minutes until the cuttlefish is tender and the sauce has thickened. Season to taste with salt and pepper.

4 Meanwhile, cook the polenta according to the package directions. When cooked, remove from the heat, stir in the parsley and season to taste with salt and pepper.

5 Transfer the polenta to 4 serving plates and top with the cuttlefish and its sauce. Garnish with a few sprigs of fresh parsley and serve.

SERVES 4

1 lb/450 g small cuttlefish, with their ink (or substitute squid)
4 tbsp olive oil
1 small onion, chopped finely
2 garlic cloves, chopped finely
1 tsp paprika, preferably Spanish
6 oz/175 g ripe tomatoes, peeled, seeded, and chopped
½ cup red wine
½ cup fish bouillon
1½ cups instant polenta
3 tbsp chopped fresh flatleaf parsley
salt and pepper

NUTRITION
Calories 430; Sugars 2 g; Protein 24 g; Carbohydrate 44 g; Fat 14 g; Saturates 2 g

 moderate

20 mins

45 mins

This is an interesting and elegant way of presenting an ordinary salmon steak.

Noisettes *of* Salmon

SERVES 4

4 salmon steaks
¼ cup butter, softened
1 garlic clove, crushed
2 tsp mustard seeds
2 tbsp chopped fresh thyme
1 tbsp chopped fresh parsley
2 tbsp vegetable oil
4 tomatoes, peeled, seeded, and chopped
salt and pepper

to serve
boiled new potatoes
green vegetables or salad greens

1 Carefully remove the central bone from the salmon steaks and cut them in half. Curl each piece round to form a medallion and tie with string. Blend the butter, garlic, mustard seeds, thyme, parsley, and seasoning together in a bowl and set aside.

2 Heat the vegetable oil in a preheated ridged griddle or skillet over medium heat. Add the salmon noisettes and brown on both sides, in batches, if necessary. Drain on paper towels and let cool.

3 Cut 4 pieces of baking parchment into 12-inch/30-cm squares. Place 2 salmon noisettes on top of each square and top with a little of the flavored butter and chopped tomato. Draw up the edges of the paper and fold together to enclose the fish. Place on a cookie sheet.

4 Cook in a preheated oven, 400°F/200°C, for 10–15 minutes or until the salmon is cooked through. Serve immediately while still warm with boiled new potatoes and a green vegetable or salad of your choice.

NUTRITION
Calories *381*; Sugars *3 g*; Protein *36 g*;
Carbohydrate *3 g*; Fat *26 g*; Saturates *4 g*

⭐⭐⭐   moderate
     20 mins
     25 mins

🍳 **COOK'S TIP**

You can make cod steaks into noisettes in the same way. Cook them with butter flavored with chives and basil.

Although the fish is quite simple to cook, a whole salmon always makes a very impressive centerpiece for any party.

Whole Poached Salmon

1 Wash the salmon under cold running water and pat dry with paper towels, then remove the fins. Place the salmon in a fish poacher or large roasting pan. Pour over the court-bouillon. Bring slowly to a boil and as soon as the liquid comes to a simmer, remove from the heat and let cool completely.

2 Meanwhile, make the watercress mayonnaise. Put the egg yolk, garlic, mustard, lemon juice, watercress, and basil into a food processor and process until the herbs are very finely chopped. Gradually add the olive oil, drop by drop, until the mixture starts to thicken. Continue adding the olive oil in a steady stream until all the oil is incorporated. Transfer to a bowl and add the scallion. Season to taste with salt and pepper. Let chill until required.

3 When the salmon is cold, carefully lift it from the poaching liquid and pat dry with paper towels. Carefully peel away and discard the skin from the rounder, uppermost side, then turn the fish and remove the skin from the flatter, underside. Slide a knife along the backbone of the fish to remove the flesh in 1 piece. Turn it over onto the serving platter so the cut side is up.

4 Remove the bones from the remaining piece of fish, then turn the remaining flesh on top of the first piece to reform the fish. Place the head and tail back on the fish to make it appear whole. Lay the cucumber slices on top of the fish, starting at the tail end, in a pattern resembling scales. Serve with the mayonnaise.

SERVES 4 – 6

3 lb 5 oz/3.5 kg salmon, cleaned and scaled
3 x quantity court-bouillon (see page 150)
½ cucumber, sliced very thinly

watercress mayonnaise

1 egg yolk
1 garlic clove, crushed
1 tsp Dijon mustard
1 tbsp lemon juice
1¾ oz/50 g watercress leaves, chopped coarsely
1 tbsp chopped fresh basil
1 cup light olive oil
1 scallion, chopped finely
salt and pepper

NUTRITION
Calories *661*; Sugars *1 g*; Protein *35 g*;
Carbohydrate *1 g*; Fat *57 g*; Saturates *9 g*

 moderate

 1 hr 15 mins

1 10 mins

This is a very impressive looking dish, which is very simple to prepare. Serve with stir-fried vegetables and boiled new potatoes.

Stuffed Monkfish Tail

SERVES 6

1 lb 10 oz/750 g monkfish tail, skinned and trimmed
6 slices prosciutto
4 tbsp chopped mixed herbs such as parsley, chives, basil, and sage
1 tsp finely grated lemon rind
2 tbsp olive oil
salt and pepper

to serve
shredded stir-fried vegetables
boiled new potatoes

NUTRITION
Calories *154*; Sugars *0 g*; Protein *24 g*; Carbohydrate *0 g*; Fat *6 g*; Saturates *1 g*

   moderate

30 mins

25 mins

1 Using a sharp knife, carefully cut down each side of the central bone of the monkfish to leave 2 fillets. Wash the fillets under cold running water and pat dry with paper towels.

2 Lay the prosciutto slices widthwise on a clean counter so that they overlap slightly. Lay the fish fillets lengthwise on top of the prosciutto so that the 2 cut sides face each other.

3 Mix the chopped herbs and lemon rind together. Season well with salt and pepper. Pack this mixture onto the cut surface of 1 monkfish fillet. Press the 2 fillets together and wrap tightly with the prosciutto slices. Secure with string or toothpicks.

4 Heat the olive oil in a large, heavy-based skillet. Place the fish in the skillet, seam side down first, and brown the wrapped monkfish tail all over.

5 Cook in a preheated oven, 400°F/200°C, for 25 minutes until golden and the fish is tender. Remove from the oven and let rest for 10 minutes before slicing thickly. Serve with shredded stir-fried vegetables and new potatoes.

 COOK'S TIP

It is possible to remove the central bone from a monkfish tail without separating the 2 fillets. This makes it easier to stuff, but takes some practice.

You could cook the lobsters on a barbecue, if you prefer. Cook them shell-side down, to protect the meat from the fierce heat of the fire and cook until nearly done then turn briefly flesh-side down.

Broiled Lobster *with* Beurre Blanc

1 Put the lobsters into the freezer for about 2 hours, then take a very large knife and cleave them in 2 pieces lengthwise behind the head. Dot the lobster flesh with the butter. Transfer to a broiler pan and cook, flesh side up, under a preheated very hot broiler for 5–7 minutes until the flesh of the lobster becomes firm and opaque.

2 Meanwhile, put the shallots into a small pan with the vinegar, white wine, and water. Bring to a boil over medium–low heat and let simmer until only 1 tablespoon of liquid remains. Reduce the heat to low and start adding the butter, a piece at a time, whisking constantly. Add the next piece of butter when the last bit has been incorporated and continue until all the butter is used and the sauce has thickened.

3 Stir in the tarragon and parsley and season to taste with salt and pepper.

4 Transfer the lobster to 4 serving plates and spoon over the beurre blanc. Garnish with lemon wedges and a few sprigs of fresh parsley and serve.

SERVES 4

4 live lobsters, about 1 lb/450 g each
2 tbsp butter

beurre blanc

1 oz/25 g shallots, chopped finely
1 tbsp white wine vinegar
1 tbsp dry white wine
¼ cup water
⅔ cup cold unsalted butter, diced
2 tsp chopped fresh tarragon
1 tbsp chopped fresh parsley
salt and pepper

to garnish
lemon wedges
fresh parsley sprigs

NUTRITION
Calories *499*; Sugars *0.5 g*; Protein *36 g*; Carbohydrate *1 g*; Fat *39 g*; Saturates *24 g*

 moderate
 2 hrs 15 mins
10 mins

COOK'S TIP

There is controversy about the most humane way to kill a lobster. It has been suggested that putting the lobsters in a freezer for 2 hours before cooking them will kill them painlessly.

This isn't really a main course dish but it would serve very well as a light lunch with some bread, or as part of a buffet.

Lobster *and* Avocado Salad

SERVES 4

2 cooked lobsters, about 14 oz/400 g each
1 large ripe avocado
1 tbsp lemon juice
8 oz/225 g green beans
4 scallions, sliced thinly
2 tbsp chopped fresh chervil
1 tbsp chopped fresh chives

dressing
1 garlic clove, crushed
1 tsp Dijon mustard
pinch of sugar
1 tbsp balsamic vinegar
5 tbsp olive oil
salt and pepper

NUTRITION
Calories *313*; Sugars *3 g*; Protein *19 g*;
Carbohydrate *4 g*; Fat *25 g*; Saturates *4 g*

   easy

25 mins

3 mins

1 To prepare the lobsters, cut them in half lengthwise. Remove the intestinal vein, which runs down the tail, stomach sack, and any gray beards from the body cavity at the head end of the lobster. Crack the claws and remove the meat—in one piece if possible. Remove the meat from the tail of each lobster. Coarsely chop all the meat and set aside.

2 Split the avocado lengthwise and remove the stone. Cut each half in half again and peel away the skin. Cut the avocado into chunks and toss with the lemon juice. Add to the lobster meat.

3 Bring a large pan of salted water to a boil over medium heat. Add the beans and cook for 3 minutes, then drain and immediately refresh under cold running water. Drain again and let cool completely. Cut the beans in half, then add to the avocado and lobster.

4 Meanwhile, make the dressing by whisking the garlic, mustard, sugar, vinegar, and seasoning together in a small bowl. Gradually add the olive oil, whisking, until thickened.

5 Add the scallions, chervil, and chives to the lobster and avocado mixture and toss gently together. Drizzle over the dressing and serve immediately.

A platter of fruits de mer is one of the most delightful of all seafood experiences. Use this recipe as a guideline and choose whatever shellfish you find on the day.

Platter *of* Fruits *de* Mer

1 To prepare the seafood, steam the mussels, clams, and cockles (if using) with just the water that clings to their shells, for 3–4 minutes until just open. Drain and refresh under cold running water. If you prefer to serve the oysters lightly cooked, scrub them and put them into a pan with just a splash of water. Cook over high heat for 3–4 minutes, drain and refresh under cold running water. Scallops should be steamed on the half shell until the flesh turns white.

2 To make the mayonnaise, put the egg yolk, mustard, lemon juice, and seasoning into a food processor and process for 30 seconds until foaming. Gradually add the olive oil, drop by drop, until the mixture starts to thicken. Continue adding the oil in a steady stream until all the oil is incorporated. Season to taste with salt and pepper, if necessary, and add a little hot water if the mixture is too thick. Let chill in the refrigerator until required.

3 To make the shallot vinaigrette, mix the vinegar, shallots, oil and seasoning together. Let stand at room temperature for 2 hours before serving.

4 To assemble the platter, place the seaweed on a large tray or platter and top with the crushed ice. Arrange the shellfish and crustaceans with the lemon wedges round the platter, sprinkling on more crushed ice as you go. Serve the mayonnaise and shallot vinaigrette separately. Don't forget to provide lobster picks, claw crackers, and finger bowls for your guests.

SERVES **6**

36 live mussels, scrubbed and bearded
18 live oysters
3 cooked lobsters, about 1 lb/450 g each
3 cooked crabs, about 1 lb 10 oz/750 g each
36 cooked langoustines or shrimp
selection of clams, cockles, and scallops
salt and pepper

mayonnaise

1 egg yolk
1 tsp Dijon mustard
1 tbsp lemon juice
2¼ cups olive oil

shallot vinaigrette

⅔ cup good-quality red wine vinegar
3 shallots, chopped finely
1 tbsp olive oil

to serve

seaweed
crushed ice
3 lemons, cut into wedges

NUTRITION

Calories *681*; Sugars *1 g*; Protein *41 g*;
Carbohydrate *3 g*; Fat *56 g*; Saturates *8 g*

 easy

2 hrs 20 mins

10–15 mins

As with many traditional French fish stews and soups, the fish and soup are served separately with a strongly flavored sauce passed around to accompany them.

Bouillabaisse

SERVES 6 – 8

5 tbsp olive oil
2 large onions, chopped finely
1 leek, chopped finely
4 garlic cloves, crushed
½ small fennel bulb, chopped finely
5 ripe tomatoes, peeled and chopped
1 fresh thyme sprig
2 strips of orange rind
6½ cups hot fish bouillon
4 lb 8oz/2 kg mixed fish, such as John Dory, sea bass, bream, red mullet, cod, skate, soft shell crabs, raw shrimp, langoustines, chopped coarsely into equal-size pieces (shellfish left whole)
12–18 thick slices French bread
salt and pepper

saffron sauce

1 red bell pepper, seeded and cut into fourths
⅔ cup light olive oil
1 egg yolk
large pinch of saffron threads
pinch of chili flakes
lemon juice, to taste

NUTRITION
Calories *844*; Sugars *10 g*; Protein *69 g*;
Carbohydrate *49 g*; Fat *43 g*; Saturates *6 g*

moderate

1 hr 15 mins

45 mins

1 To make the red bell pepper and saffron sauce. Brush the red pepper fourths with a little of the olive oil. Place under a preheated hot broiler and cook for 5–6 minutes on each side until the skin is charred and blistered and the flesh is tender. Place the bell pepper in a plastic bag until cool enough to handle, then peel off the skins.

2 Place the bell pepper into a food processor with the egg yolk, saffron, chili flakes, lemon juice, and seasoning and process until smooth. Gradually add the remaining olive oil, drop by drop, until the mixture starts to thicken. Continue adding the oil in a steady stream until all the oil is incorporated and the mixture is thick. Add a little hot water if it is too thick.

3 Heat the olive oil in a large pan over low heat. Add the onions, leek, garlic, and fennel and cook for 10–15 minutes until softened and starting to color. Add the tomatoes, thyme, orange rind, and salt and pepper to taste, and cook for another 5 minutes until the tomatoes have collapsed.

4 Add the fish bouillon and bring to a boil over medium heat. Let simmer gently for 10 minutes until all the vegetables are tender. Add the fish and return to a boil. Let simmer gently for 10 minutes until all the fish is tender.

5 When the soup is ready, toast the bread on both sides, then divide the fish among 4 serving plates. Add some of the soup to moisten the stew and serve with the toast. Serve the sauce and the remaining soup separately.

Soufflés are always impressive and this one is no exception. Serve straight from the oven but don't worry if it sinks en route to the table—it's the nature of the beast.

Crab Soufflé

1 Generously butter a 5-cup soufflé dish. Add the bread crumbs and shake around the dish to coat completely, shaking out any excess. Set aside on a large cookie sheet.

2 Melt the butter in a large pan over low heat. Add the onion and cook gently for 8 minutes until softened, but not colored. Add the garlic and cook for another 1 minute. Add the mustard powder and flour and cook for 1 minute. Gradually add the milk, stirring constantly, until smooth. Increase the heat slightly and bring slowly to a boil, stirring constantly. Let simmer gently for 2 minutes. Remove from the heat and stir in the cheese. Let cool slightly.

3 Lightly beat in the egg yolks, then fold in the crabmeat, chives, cayenne, and season generously with salt and pepper.

4 Whisk the egg whites in a clean bowl until stiff peaks form. Add 1 large spoonful of the egg whites to the crab mixture and fold together to slacken. Add the remaining egg whites and fold together carefully, but thoroughly. Spoon into the prepared dish.

5 Cook in a preheated oven, 400°F/200°C, for 25 minutes until well risen and golden. Serve immediately.

COOK'S TIP

Place a baking sheet in the oven to preheat before cooking the soufflé. This helps keep the soufflé to rise.

SERVES 4 – 6

¼ cup butter, plus 1 tbsp for greasing
¼ cup dried bread crumbs
1 small onion, chopped finely
1 garlic clove, crushed
2 tsp mustard powder
¼ cup all-purpose flour
1 cup milk
1¾ oz/50 g hard Swiss cheese, grated
3 eggs, separated
8 oz/225 g fresh crabmeat, thawed if frozen
2 tbsp chopped fresh chives
pinch of cayenne pepper
salt and pepper

NUTRITION
Calories 214; Sugars 1 g; Protein 15 g; Carbohydrate 8 g; Fat 14 g; Saturates 7 g

moderate

15 mins

35 mins

This is very nice served with the Quick Tomato Sauce that accompanies the Tuna Fish Cakes on page 103.

Spinach Roulade

SERVES 4

8 oz/225 g frozen spinach, thawed and well-drained
2 tbsp butter
¼ cup all-purpose flour
¾ cup milk
4 eggs, separated
1 tbsp chopped fresh tarragon
½ tsp freshly grated nutmeg
1 tbsp olive oil, for brushing
salt and pepper

filling

12 oz/350 g skinless smoked cod fillet
4 oz/115 g ricotta cheese
1 oz/25 g freshly grated Parmesan cheese
4 scallions, chopped finely
2 tbsp freshly chopped chives
1¾ oz/50 g sun-dried tomatoes in olive oil, drained and finely chopped

NUTRITION
Calories *331*; Sugars *5 g*; Protein *27 g*;
Carbohydrate *10 g*; Fat *21 g*; Saturates *9 g*

moderate

25 mins

40 mins

1 Grease a 13 x 9-inch/33 x 23-cm jelly roll pan and then line with baking parchment. Squeeze the spinach to remove as much liquid as possible. Chop finely and set aside.

2 Melt the butter in a small pan over low heat. Add the flour and cook for 30 seconds, stirring. Gradually add the milk, stirring constantly, until smooth. Bring slowly to a boil and let simmer for 2 minutes, stirring. Remove from the heat and let cool slightly.

3 Stir in the spinach, egg yolks, tarragon, nutmeg, and salt and pepper to taste. Whisk the egg whites until stiff peaks form. Fold 1 large spoonful into the spinach mixture to slacken it, then fold in the remaining egg whites, carefully, but thoroughly to avoid losing any volume. Pour the mixture into the prepared pan and smooth the surface.

4 Cook in a preheated oven, 400°F/200°C, for 15 minutes until risen and golden and firm in the center. Turn out immediately onto a clean dishtowel, peel off the baking parchment and roll up from one short end.

5 To make the filling, cover the fillet with boiling water and let stand for 10 minutes until just tender. Remove the fish and flake carefully, removing any bones, and mix with the ricotta, Parmesan cheese, scallions, chives, sun-dried tomatoes, and salt and pepper to taste.

6 Unroll the roulade and spread with the cod leaving a 1-inch/2.5-cm border all around. Re-roll and return to the oven, seam side down, for 20 minutes.

This is definitely a fish pie for impressing the guests! Serve piping hot with boiled new potatoes and a selection of freshly cooked vegetables.

Luxury Fish Pie

1 To make the filling, melt 2 tablespoons of the butter in a skillet over high heat. Add the shallots and cook for 5 minutes until softened. Add the mushrooms and cook for 2 minutes. Add the wine and let simmer until the liquid has evaporated. Transfer to a 6¼-cup shallow ovenproof dish.

2 Put the mussels into a large pan with just the water that clings to their shells and cook, covered, over high heat for 3–4 minutes until all the mussels have opened. Discard any that remain closed. Strain, reserving the cooking liquid. Remove the mussels from their shells and add to the mushrooms.

3 Bring the court-bouillon to a boil over low heat. Add the monkfish and poach for 2 minutes before adding the cod, sole, and shrimp. Poach for 2 minutes. Remove the fish with a draining spoon and add to the mussels.

4 Melt the remaining butter in a pan over low heat. Add the flour and stir until smooth, then cook for 2 minutes without coloring. Gradually, stir in the hot court-bouillon and mussel cooking liquid until smooth and thickened. Add the cream and let simmer gently for 15 minutes, stirring. Season to taste with salt and pepper and pour over the fish.

5 Meanwhile, make the topping. Bring a pan of water to a boil over medium heat. Add the potatoes and cook for 15–20 minutes until tender. Drain and mash with the butter, egg yolks, milk, nutmeg and seasoning. Pipe over the fish and roughen the surface of the topping with a fork. Bake the fish pie in a preheated oven, 400°F/200°C, for 30 minutes until golden and bubbling. Garnish with fresh parsley and serve.

SERVES 4

½ cup butter
3 shallots, chopped finely
2 cups button mushrooms, halved
2 tbsp dry white wine
2 lb/900 g live mussels, scrubbed and bearded
1 x quantity court-bouillon (see page 150)
10½ oz/300 g monkfish fillet, cubed
10½ oz/300 g skinless cod fillet, cubed
10½ oz/300 g skinless lemon sole fillet, cubed
4 oz/115 g jumbo shrimp, peeled
¼ cup all-purpose flour
¼ cup heavy cream

potato topping
3 lb 5oz/1.5 kg floury potatoes, cut into chunks
¼ cup butter
2 egg yolks
½ cup milk
pinch of freshly grated nutmeg
salt and pepper
fresh parsley sprigs, to garnish

NUTRITION
Calories *863*; Sugars *5 g*; Protein *66 g*;
Carbohydrate *60 g*; Fat *41 g*; Saturates *24 g*

 moderate
 1 hr 10 mins
1 hr 10 mins

This is a really delicious and filling dish. Layers of potato slices and mixed fish are cooked in a creamy sauce and topped with grated cheese.

Layered Fish *and* Potato Pie

SERVES 4

2 lb/900 g waxy potatoes, peeled and sliced
5 tbsp butter
1 red onion, halved and sliced
5 tbsp all-purpose flour
2 cups milk
½ cup heavy cream
8 oz/225 g smoked haddock fillet, cubed
8 oz/225 g cod fillet, cubed
1 red bell pepper, seeded and diced
4 oz/115 g broccoli florets
½ cup freshly grated Parmesan cheese
salt and pepper

1 Bring a large pan of lightly salted water to a boil over medium heat. Add the sliced potatoes and cook for 10 minutes. Drain and set aside.

2 Meanwhile, melt the butter in a pan over low heat. Add the onion and cook gently for 3–4 minutes.

3 Add the flour and cook, stirring, for 1 minute. Blend in the milk and cream and bring to a boil, stirring constantly, until the sauce has thickened.

4 Arrange half of the potato slices in the bottom of a shallow ovenproof dish.

5 Add the fish, red bell pepper and broccoli to the sauce and cook over low heat for 10 minutes. Season to taste with salt and pepper, then spoon the mixture over the potatoes in the dish.

6 Arrange the remaining potato slices in a layer over the fish mixture and then sprinkle the Parmesan cheese over the top.

7 Cook in a preheated oven, 350°F/180°C, for 30 minutes or until the potatoes are cooked and the topping is golden.

NUTRITION
Calories 116; Sugars 1.9 g; Protein 6.2 g;
Carbohydrate 9.7 g; Fat 6.1 g; Saturates 3.8 g

 easy

 10 mins

10 mins

55 mins

COOK'S TIP

Vary the fish according to personal taste and availability. Do use fillets and remove as many of the bones as possible.

This pie is simplicity itself and can be prepared in advance and reheated just before serving.

Salmon *and* Zucchini Pie

1 Heat the oil in a pan over low heat. Add the bell peppers, onion and a little seasoning and cook for 10–15 minutes until softened. Transfer to a food processor or blender and process until smooth or rub through a fine strainer.

2 Bring a small pan of water to a boil over medium heat. Add the eggs and cook for 10 minutes from when the water returns to a boil, then refresh under cold running water. When cool enough to handle, drain and shell.

3 Coarsely chop the eggs and add to the pepper purée with the salmon, zucchini, dill, and seasoning. Mix well and set aside.

4 To make the pie dough, put the flour into a bowl with ½ teaspoon of salt. Add the butter and rub it in with your fingertips until the mixture resembles fine bread crumbs. Add the egg yolks with enough cold water to make a firm dough. Turn onto a lightly floured counter and knead briefly until smooth.

5 Roll out a little over half of the dough and use to line a 9-inch/23-cm pie plate. Fill with the salmon mixture and dampen the edges with a little water. Roll out the remaining dough and use to cover the pie, pinching the edges to seal. Make a cross or slash in the top of the pie for steam to escape. Re-roll any trimmings, cut into fish tails or leaf shapes and use to decorate the edges of the pie, attaching them with a little beaten egg or milk. Brush more egg or milk over the rest of the pie to glaze.

6 Bake in a preheated oven, 400°F/200°C, for 35–40 minutes until the pie dough is golden. Garnish with Chinese garlic and serve.

SERVES 4

2 tbsp olive oil
2 red bell peppers, seeded and chopped
1 medium onion, chopped finely
2 eggs
8 oz/225 g salmon fillet, skinned and cubed
1 zucchini, sliced
1 tsp chopped fresh dill
salt and pepper
Chinese garlic, to garnish

pie dough
3 cups all-purpose flour, plus extra
    for dusting
½ tsp salt
¾ cup cold butter, diced
2 egg yolks
3–4 tbsp cold water
beaten egg or milk, to glaze

NUTRITION
Calories *902*; Sugars *9 g*; Protein *28 g*;
Carbohydrate *77 g*; Fat *56 g*; Saturates *28 g*

★★★ moderate

 40 mins

 1 hr 10 mins

Hot-smoked trout is available from fish markets and some large supermarkets. The fish is smoked in a hot environment, which cooks the flesh as well as flavoring it.

Hot-Smoked Trout Tart

SERVES 6

1½ cups all-purpose flour, plus extra to dust
1 tsp salt
⅓ cup butter, cut into small pieces
2–3 tbsp cold water
1 egg yolk

filling

2 tbsp butter
1 small onion, chopped finely
1 tsp green peppercorns in brine, drained
    and coarsely chopped
2 tsp candied ginger, drained
2 tsp candied ginger syrup
8 oz/225 g hot-smoked trout fillets, flaked
3 egg yolks
scant ½ cup crème fraîche or
    mascarpone cheese
scant ½ cup heavy cream
1 tbsp chopped fresh parsley
1 tbsp chopped fresh chives
salt and pepper
lemon slices, to garnish
mixed salad greens, to serve

NUTRITION

Calories *650*; Sugars *6 g*; Protein *22 g*;
Carbohydrate *40 g*; Fat *46 g*; Saturates *27 g*

⭐⭐⭐   moderate

🕐   1 hr 10 mins

🕐   1 hr 20 mins

1 Strain the flour and salt together into a bowl. Add the butter and rub it in with your fingertips until the mixture resembles coarse bread crumbs. Add the egg yolk and enough cold water to make a firm dough. Knead briefly, wrap in plastic wrap and let chill in the refrigerator for 30 minutes.

2 Meanwhile, make the filling. Melt the butter in a skillet over low heat. Add the onion and cook gently for 8–10 minutes until softened, but not colored. Remove from the heat and stir in the peppercorns, ginger, ginger syrup, and flaked trout. Set aside.

3 Remove the dough from the refrigerator and roll out thinly on a lightly floured counter. Use to line a 9-inch/23-cm tart pan. Prick the bottom at regular intervals with a fork. Line the dough with foil or baking parchment and baking beans. Bake in a preheated oven, 400°F/200°C, for 12 minutes. Remove the foil or baking parchment and beans and bake for another 10 minutes until light golden and dry. Remove from the oven and let cool slightly. Reduce the oven temperature to 350°F/180°C. Spread the trout mixture over the bottom of the baked pie shell.

4 Mix the egg yolks, crème fraîche, cream, parsley, chives, and seasoning together. Pour this mixture over the trout mixture to cover. Bake in the preheated oven for 35–40 minutes until just set and golden. Remove from the oven and let cool slightly. Transfer to 4 large serving plates, garnish with lemon slices and serve with mixed salad greens.

Smoked haddock gives this tart a deliciously savory flavor. Serve with salad greens, if desired.

Smoked Haddock *and* Spinach Tart

1 To make the pie dough, mix both flours together in a bowl with the salt. Add the butter and rub it in with your fingertips until the mixture resembles fine bread crumbs. Stir in enough cold water to form a firm dough. Knead the dough briefly until the surface is smooth.

2 Roll out the dough thinly on a lightly floured counter and use to line an 8-inch/20-cm deep fluted flan pan. Put the lined pan in the freezer for 15 minutes. Line with foil or baking parchment and baking beans and place in a preheated oven, 400°F/200°C, for 10–12 minutes. Remove the foil or parchment and beans and bake for another 10 minutes until pale golden and dry. Let cool slightly. Reduce the oven temperature to 375°F/190°C.

3 To make the filling, place the haddock in a skillet, cover with milk and cream. Bring to a boil over medium–high heat, cover and remove from heat. Let stand for 10 minutes until the haddock is tender. Remove the fish with a draining spoon. Strain the cooking liquid into a jug. Skin and flake the fish.

4 Press the spinach in a strainer or squeeze well to remove excess liquid. Arrange the spinach in the pie shell with the flaked fish. Add the egg yolks to the fish poaching liquid along with ½ cup of the cheese and salt and pepper to taste. Mix and pour into the pie shell. Sprinkle over the remaining cheese and bake in the preheated oven for 25–30 minutes until the filling is risen, golden and just set.

SERVES 6

⅔ cup whole-wheat flour
⅔ cup all-purpose flour, plus extra
    for dusting
pinch of salt
½ cup chilled butter, diced
2–2 tbsp cold water

filling
12 oz/350 g smoked haddock fillet
⅔ cup plus 2 tbsp milk
⅔ cup plus 2 tbsp heavy cream
4 oz/115 g frozen leaf spinach, thawed
3 egg yolks, beaten lightly
3 oz/85 g mature sharp cheese, grated
salt and pepper

NUTRITION
Calories *458*; Sugars *3 g*; Protein *23 g*;
Carbohydrate *21 g*; Fat *32 g*; Saturates *19 g*

 moderate

 45 mins

    1 hr 10 mins

Index